SCANDINAVIA

DENMARK

ICELAND

NORWAY

FINLAND

SWEDEN

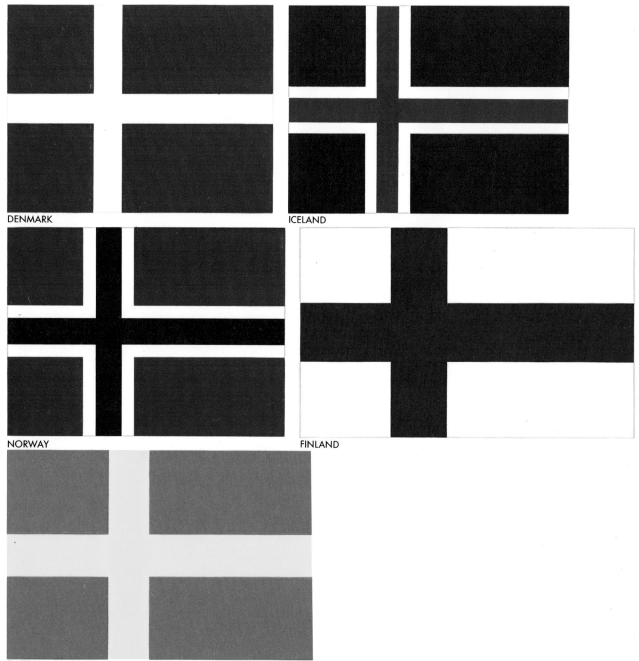

DENMARK

ICELAND

NORWAY

FINLAND

SWEDEN

SCANDINAVIA

By the Editors of Time-Life Books

TIME-LIFE BOOKS · AMSTERDAM

TIME-LIFE HISTORY OF THE WORLD
FITNESS, HEALTH & NUTRITION
HEALTHY HOME COOKING
UNDERSTANDING COMPUTERS
THE ENCHANTED WORLD
LIBRARY OF NATIONS
HOME REPAIR AND IMPROVEMENT
CLASSICS OF EXPLORATION
PLANET EARTH
PEOPLES OF THE WILD
THE EPIC OF FLIGHT
THE SEAFARERS
WORLD WAR II
THE GOOD COOK
THE TIME-LIFE ENCYCLOPAEDIA
OF GARDENING
THE GREAT CITIES
THE OLD WEST
THE WORLD'S WILD PLACES
THE EMERGENCE OF MAN
LIFE LIBRARY OF PHOTOGRAPHY
TIME-LIFE LIBRARY OF ART
GREAT AGES OF MAN
LIFE SCIENCE LIBRARY
LIFE NATURE LIBRARY
THE TIME-LIFE BOOK OF BOATING
TECHNIQUES OF PHOTOGRAPHY
LIFE AT WAR
LIFE GOES TO THE MOVIES
BEST OF LIFE
LIFE IN SPACE

TIME-LIFE BOOKS

EUROPEAN EDITOR: Kit van Tulleken
Assistant European Editor: Gillian Moore
Design Director: Ed Skyner
Chief of Research: Vanessa Kramer
Chief Sub-Editor: Ilse Gray

LIBRARY OF NATIONS

Series Editor: Tony Allan

Editorial Staff for *Scandinavia*
Editor: John Cottrell
Deputy Editor: Ellen Galford
Researcher: Susan Dawson
Designer: Mary Staples
Sub-Editor: Sally Rowland
Picture Department: Christine Hinze, Peggy Tout
Editorial Assistant: Molly Oates

EDITORIAL PRODUCTION

Chief: Jane Hawker
Production Assistants: Alan Godwin, Maureen Kelly
Editorial Department: Theresa John, Debra Lelliott,
Sylvia Osborne

CONSULTANT: Dr. W.R. Mead is Professor Emeritus of Geography at University College, London. He has written several books on Scandinavia, among them *An Historical Geography of Scandinavia* and *An Economic Geography of the Scandinavian Countries and Finland.*

Special Contributors: The chapter texts were written by: Windsor Chorlton, Michael Frenchman, Frederic V. Grunfeld, W.R. Mead and Barry Turner.
Other contributors: Patricia Clough and Hazel Evans.

Cover: Three pedestrians warmly wrapped against the winter cold make their way past the modern Tromsdalen Church in Tromsø, northern Norway. Built of concrete and glass, the structure is known as the "Cathedral of the Arctic".

Front and back endpapers: A topographic map showing the major rivers, lakes, mountain ranges and other natural features of Scandinavia appears on the front endpaper. The back endpaper shows the five countries of Scandinavia, with the principal towns and islands.

This volume is one in a series of books describing countries of the world—their natural resources, peoples, histories, economies and governments.

CONTENTS

A glowing sun, still hovering above the horizon at 1 o'clock in the morning, casts an eerie light over Reisafjord in northern Norway. The "midnight sun",

BIG LANDS WITH SPACE TO SPARE

The bulk of Scandinavia's land area, which totals 1,257,284 square kilometres—about the size of the EEC countries, excluding Greece—is taken up by Sweden, Finland and Norway, respectively the fourth, fifth and sixth biggest states in Europe. Large areas of each country are sparsely inhabited, however, so population density figures are low—a characteristic even more evident in Iceland, which averages just 2 people per square kilometre. Only smaller, intensively cultivated Denmark has a density approaching the crowded Western European norm.

	ICELAND	NORWAY	FINLAND	DENMARK	SWEDEN	
	237,000	4·1 million	4·8 million	5·1 million	8·3 million	Population
	2	13	14	118	19	Population density (persons per sq. km.)
	103,000	324,219	337,032	43,069	449,964	Area (in sq. kms.)
	Reykjavik	Oslo	Helsinki	Copenhagen	Stockholm	Capital

visible in midsummer in districts north of the Arctic Circle only, is one of the strangest and most distinctive features of the Scandinavian world.

WINTERS TEMPERED BY THE SEA

	°C
Mean temperature in mid-January	
0 to 4	
−4 to 0	
−8 to −4	
−12 to −8	
−16 to −12	

	°C
Moscow	−9·9
Helsinki	−5·4
Oslo	−4·7
Stockholm	−2·9
Berlin	−0·5
Reykjavik	−0·4
Copenhagen	0·1
New York	0·9
Tokyo	3·7
London	4·2

In spite of its northerly location, much of Scandinavia experiences relatively mild winters, as shown in the chart on the left, which compares January mean temperatures in various northern cities. In the west, this mildness is due to the relatively warm currents of the North Atlantic Drift and accompanying westerly winds, which keep the tidal, salty waters around Iceland, Denmark, Norway and south-west Sweden free of ice. To the east, however, high pressure ridges forming over Eastern Europe cause the brackish waters of the Gulfs of Bothnia and Finland to freeze over. As a result, the north of Sweden and Finland are the coldest parts of the area in winter.

Warmly wrapped against the snow, a woman basks in the sun beside an annexe

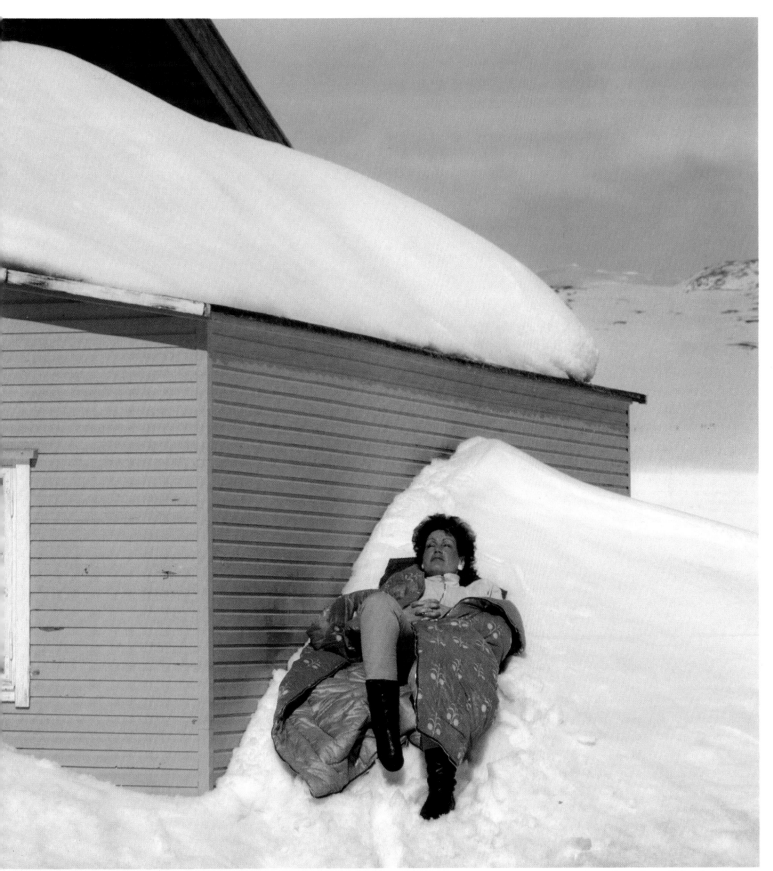

to her wooden holiday cabin in Mörkedalen, a valley in southern Norway popular with skiers during the longer, late-winter days of March and April.

Seabirds flock around a trawler off the Westman Islands, south of Iceland. Although only 5 per cent of Iceland's work force are fishermen, their catch

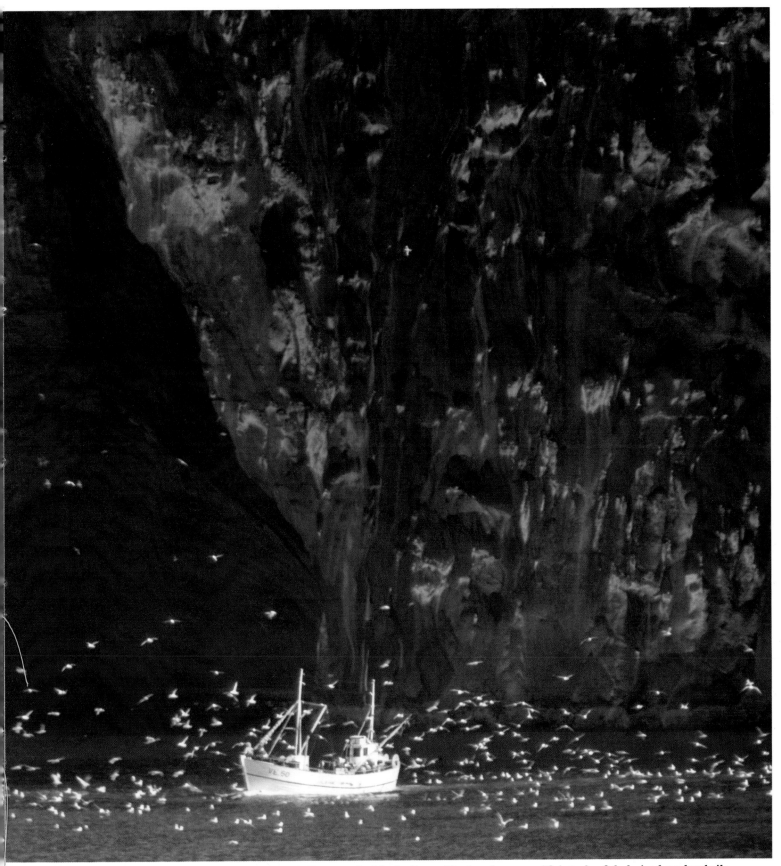

provides the raw material for about three quarters of all exports both in the form of fresh and preserved fish, and as fish-derived meal and oils.

A HIGH STANDARD OF LIVING WIDELY SHARED

Thriving economies and an egalitarian spread of wealth—the income of a Swedish cabinet minister in 1984 was only about double that of a factory worker—have ensured a high standard of living for most Scandinavians. Figures for gross national product per capita are among the highest in the world. Sweden, once second in international terms only to Switzerland, was overtaken in the early 1980s by Norway, as the latter began to benefit from the exploitation of its North Sea oil and gas fields. Denmark at that time stood fifth and Finland 11th in the personal income league.

Such shared affluence has meant that expensive consumer goods such as colour TVs, refrigerators, freezers and cars are expected possessions for most Scandinavian families. Second homes, too, are increasingly common. Norwegians, for example, owned 300,000 holiday homes in 1984—one for every five households—as well as a quarter of a million pleasure boats. Nor is public spending neglected: a large proportion of personal income is diverted through taxation to finance social services that are among the most comprehensive in the world.

On an island in the Stockholm archipelago, two young women relax outside a holiday home. Behind them stands a sauna with a stockpile of wood stored

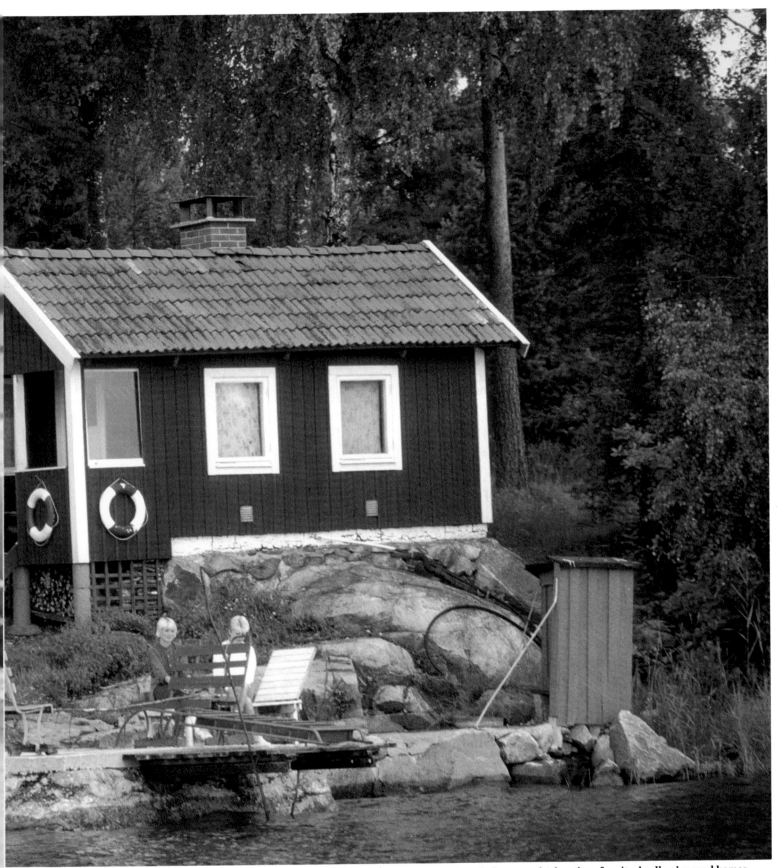

underneath it. The thousands of small islands that dot the Baltic to the east of the Swedish capital are popular locations for city dwellers' second homes.

Water from the River Lågen, swollen by rain, pours through the floodgates of the Hunderfossen Dam, a hydroelectric power plant near Lillehammer in

DENMARK　FINLAND　SWEDEN　ICELAND　NORWAY

50

100

HYDROPOWER (as percentage of total electricity production)

POWER FROM THE RIVERS

Water is the most important resource for generating electricity in Norway, Iceland and Sweden, where fast-flowing rivers have encouraged the building of hydroelectric power stations. In Norway, indeed, hydropower meets 99.8 per cent of electricity demand, and the figure is almost as high in Iceland, even though only about 10 per cent of the island's available water resources are exploited. Most of Sweden's hydroelectric potential is already developed; to meet extra demand, the nation currently depends chiefly on nuclear energy. Finland also gets much of its supply from nuclear reactors, while Denmark relies almost entirely on imported coal and oil to feed its electricity grid.

southern Norway. Most of the nation's hydropower schemes are sited in the south, where the rainfall is heavier.

A UNION OF NATIONS

Encircled by sea and hills, the port of
Ålesund on Norway's rugged west
coast is one of many Scandinavian
settlements that are intricately bound
to waterside settings. The majority of
Nordic people live close to the sea or
beside rivers or lakes.

In the first century A.D., when writing
his monumental *Historia Naturalis*, the
Roman encyclopaedist Pliny the Elder
made the first known reference to Scandinavia. Beyond indicating that it lay
in north-western Europe, he failed to
define the region clearly; and now,
nearly 2,000 years later, there is still
confusion and disagreement about its
true definition. Some geographers argue that it is purely and simply the huge
mountainous peninsula shared by
Norway and Sweden. Traditionalists
tend to see it as a trio of ancient kingdoms—Denmark, Norway and Swe-
den—which were once united under a
single crown. More usually, however,
the name is applied abroad to Denmark, Finland, Iceland, Norway and
Sweden—five nations linked by reli-
gious, historical and geographical ties,
and now bound together more closely
than any other group of politically independent countries.

The functional integration within
the frontiers of Scandinavia is unique
in the world. Under the terms of the
1962 Helsinki Treaty, these five Nordic
states—who prefer the term "Norden"
to describe their collective presence—
undertake to maintain and develop co-
operation in legal, cultural, social and
economic fields. They have a common
postage rate and increasingly harmon-
ized industrial, commercial, legal and
educational systems. They constitute a
common labour market and a common
passport area, being integrated to such

a degree that Danes, Finns, Icelanders,
Norwegians and Swedes enjoy a remarkable degree of mutual citizenship, and
they have almost as much freedom of
movement and settlement as Americans have within the 50 states of the
United States.

The extent of this Scandinavian co-
operation was dramatically illustrated
on September 3, 1967—the so-called
H-Day ("H" for *hoger*, meaning
right)—when Sweden made the switch
to driving on the right-hand side of the
road to conform with the neighbouring
Nordic partners. For more than two
centuries, left-side traffic had been the
official practice in Sweden. But in 1963
the government decided to make a
change, even though it involved years
of preparation at a cost of 600 million
kronur (then about £48 million). The
following year, Iceland also switched
to the right, so completing Nordic harmony in traffic procedures.

Ostensibly, such a degree of Nordic
conformity is extraordinary when one
considers that Scandinavia's 22.5 million inhabitants are scattered far and
wide over lands variously separated by
the Baltic Sea, the North Sea and the
Atlantic Ocean. Iceland, the most isolated country in Europe, lies some 900
kilometres from the peninsula of Norway and Sweden. Excluding the icy
wastes of Greenland, officially a consti-
tuent part of Denmark though now self-
governing, Scandinavia has a land
area of 1,257,284 square kilometres,

greater than Britain, France and West Germany combined.

On the other hand, geography contributes in many ways to the sense of community felt by the Nordic countries. All are high-latitude lands on the north-west fringe of Europe. All of them suffer high costs in maintaining their communications systems because of the nature of their topography and, Denmark excepted, because of the severity of their winters. All five countries possess a limited variety of natural resources, though some of these resources—for example, timber in Finland and Sweden—are abundant. All have relatively small populations and, again with the exception of Denmark, have vast wilderness areas.

Historically, the five Nordic countries were first united in 1397 when Queen Margrethe of Denmark established the Union of Kalmar, joining Denmark, Norway and Sweden, along with their dependencies of Iceland and Finland, under one crown. The union

both Iceland and Finland have an elected president as their head of state. This, however, is only a cosmetic difference. Fundamentally, all the countries are Western-style parliamentary democracies that are governed by propor-

formally ended with the secession of Sweden in 1523. However, Norway and Denmark (then including Iceland and the Faeroe Islands) remained united for several centuries under a single monarchy; and Finland had six and a half centuries of close association with Sweden before being ceded to Russia in 1809 and becoming a Grand Duchy.

In social terms, too, the Nordic countries have developed many common characteristics. The five countries are now urbanized and, Iceland apart, they have modern industrial and service economies. All have egalitarian societies, advanced social security systems and very high living standards. Denmark, Norway and Sweden are constitutional monarchies, whereas

tional representation; and all have so many well-supported political parties that coalition governments prevail.

Scandinavians are also linked by the Lutheran religion—to which 95 per cent of the population of the five countries nominally adhere—and by close linguistic ties shared by the Danes, Swedes, Icelanders and Norwegians. Finnish belongs to a totally different language group. However, Finland is officially bilingual, and most Finns

The faces of a random collection of Scandinavians, from a Norwegian woman to an old, bearded Lapp, reveal that despite the popular stereotype of blond hair and blue eyes the northern lands actually house a diversity of peoples and physiognomies.

have some understanding of their second language, Swedish, which is a compulsory subject in secondary schools. Moreover, when Scandinavians are unable to communicate in one of their own languages, English—taught to virtually all schoolchildren—usually bridges the gap.

Scandinavian unity on a significant scale dates from 1952, with the establishment of the Nordic Council, an organ set up by Norway, Sweden,

Denmark and Iceland for co-operation between their governments. Finland became a member in 1955. More recently, Denmark's Atlantic outposts, Greenland and the Faeroe Islands, together with the Åland Islands (an autonomous province of Finland in the Baltic) have been granted the right to nominate their own representatives.

The first significant achievements of the Nordic Council came in 1954 when the member countries agreed to a common labour market, which enabled their nationals to work and settle in any of the signatory lands without a work permit or a permanent resident's visa. Since then, more than one million persons have migrated from one Nordic country to another, the greatest flow being from Finland into Sweden.

Additional examples of Nordic co-operation include collaboration in the use of transatlantic satellite links, in the exchange and production of television programmes, in tackling environmen-

tal problems, in constructing interstate highways and bridges, in jointly awarding prizes for the arts and in making grants for translating literary works from one Scandinavian language into another. A joint airline company, the Scandinavian Airlines System, or SAS, is operated by public and private capital from Denmark, Norway and Sweden. The power systems of Denmark, Finland, Norway and Sweden are interconnected so that surpluses of electricity can be transferred across their borders. There is also close cooperation between trade unions, sports and youth associations, and Nordic Societies—groups working in each country to promote better understanding between Scandinavian states.

In addition, the Nordic countries coordinate regional planning in certain border areas where they may share services such as municipal fire brigades, schools and hospitals, and they work together in respect of their common interests such as tourism, road construc-

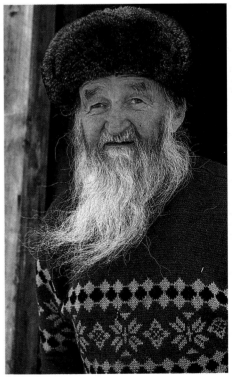

1

tion and communications. No part of Scandinavia stands to benefit more from this arrangement than those provinces of Finland, Norway and Sweden that are situated partly or entirely within the Arctic Circle. In this region—known as Nordkalotten because its cartographic shape resembles the calotte, or skullcap, worn by a priest— some 930,000 inhabitants are widely scattered over a mostly barren area of about 305,000 square kilometres, and very often far removed from centres of supply and demand.

The other main area of co-ordinated planning in Scandinavia is the Øresund: a Danish-Swedish metropolitan region with a population of 2.8 million, which embraces both sides of the Sound, the narrow channel of water that separates Denmark and south-west Sweden. In 1964, a Dano-Swedish Øresund Council was established to consider matters of mutual interest, including pollution problems and joint development of cultural and leisure amenities. Plans for integrating the Øresund conurbation include the construction of a bridge over the Sound, connecting the Copenhagen area and the south-west coast of Sweden.

Over the years, this unusually close family of five nations has suffered its share of shocks and set-backs, most conspicuously in respect of trading agreements. In 1947, a Scandinavian customs union was proposed, then rejected. In 1970, a Danish initiative for a Nordic common market was turned down by the Finns because of their economic links with the Soviet Union. Three years later, Denmark joined the European Common Market (EEC) and Finland signed trade treaties with Comecon, the council for mutual economic assistance among socialist coun-

tries that was founded in 1949.

However, despite this divergence, the Nordic countries continue to have strong trading links, especially by way of the European Free Trade Association (EFTA), founded in 1959. Denmark, Norway, Sweden and Iceland are members of EFTA, and Finland has been an associate member since 1961. This trading alliance has been a key factor in the increase of intra-Nordic trade, which has grown twice as fast as Nordic foreign trade. To a lesser degree, the EEC also represents a trading link; only Denmark is a member, but all the other Nordic countries have concluded bilateral agreements with the community.

There is less uniformity in the crucial area of defence. In 1948, Sweden proposed the formation of a Scandinavian Defence Union that would have required the declared neutrality of all member countries, with a commitment to defend any member nation attacked by a third party. Denmark supported the proposal at first, but later came to share the view of Norway and Iceland (both of whom had proclaimed their neutrality in World War II with absolutely no effect) that such a union would offer them no real protection in the event of a major conflict. Meanwhile, Finland had signed a Treaty of Friendship, Co-operation and Mutual Assistance with the Soviet Union. This treaty leaves the defence of Finland to Finnish armed forces, but it allows for the possibility of military aid from either party if the other country is attacked by Germany, or countries allied to Germany.

Closer bonds between the countries are discouraged by the fact that, while the Nordic peoples have a strong sense of kinship, they also passionately cher-

ish their individualism and national independence. Throughout Scandinavia, national pride is evinced by the ubiquitous show of flags—on harbour fronts and at airports, on yachts and motor boats, at hotel entrances and on dinner tables, both public and private. Even the Faeroes and the Åland Islands have their own territorial flags. By contrast, there is no flag for Norden as a whole. Instead, at Nordic Council meetings, a row of national flags flying side by side are seen as preferable to a single emblem.

Gylfi Gíslason, a former Icelandic Minister of Education and member of the Nordic Council, has explained: "Each nation has nurtured a strong patriotism that it is careful to preserve. Each considers the present collaboration no obstacle to these feelings; on the contrary, it is an encouragement. Thus it is no wonder that proposals for a Nordic state or union of states are invariably rejected, since no advantage that would accrue from such an alliance could be more important than the preservation of the culture and nationality of each individual state." Quite simply, although a remarkable degree of harmony exists, each Scandinavian state is a unique entity, steeped in its own mythologies, its inhabitants harbouring emotions born of experiences particular to the terrains and territories of their homelands.

Of all the Scandinavian countries, Denmark is the most markedly different from the rest. It is by far the smallest—a mere 43,069 square kilometres, less than one fifth the size of the United Kingdom. It is the most low-lying, its highest point being just 173 metres above sea level, and it has the mildest climate and the most amenable soils.

A global view of the northernmost latitudes reveals the full extent of the Scandinavian world, here coloured yellow. The map takes in the five Nordic countries, plus Greenland, the Svalbard archipelago and the Faeroes, all politically part of Scandinavia.

Furthermore, it is the oldest inhabited part of Scandinavia (man is known to have lived there for at least 10,000 years); the most densely populated, with roughly 118 Danes to the square kilometre; and the most urban with more than 80 per cent of its 5.1 million inhabitants living in cities or towns.

Denmark has a highly humanized landscape. Approximately 70 per cent of its surface area is farmed, and another 10 per cent is taken up by well-ordered woodland. It has heaths, bogs, dunes and salt marshes, but, unlike the rest of Scandinavia, it is predominantly well tended and without any truly wild, untameable land. Nor, for that matter, is the country rich in natural resources beyond its farmland and coastal fisheries. The only basic raw materials are clay and chalk—the foundation of cement and brick-making industries. In recent years, Denmark has gained a small share in the North Sea oil and natural gas fields. Otherwise it is virtually devoid of mineral wealth.

The differences between Denmark and other Nordic countries extend to the people. The Danes tend to be more cosmopolitan in their attitudes and lifestyles. In part, this is explained by their country's location at major cross-roads of international trade. The Danes live beside the North Sea's narrow gateway to the Baltic Sea, and their territory has always provided island stepping-stones between central and northern Europe. As a result, its inhabitants have been subject to foreign intrusion, influence and intermarriage.

Denmark is a highly fragmented country. It is made up of the northern half of the peninsula of Jutland, together with 406 separate islands, of which Zealand and Funen are the largest. Ninety-seven of the islands are in-habited, and no Dane lives more than 52 kilometres from the sea. The Danish capital Copenhagen is located on the east coast of Zealand, within sight of Skåne, Sweden's southernmost province, which was once part of the king-dom of Denmark.

The West German federal state, or *Land*, of Schleswig-Holstein, constituting the southern part of the Jutland peninsula, was also formerly a part of the Danish realm. But now it is separated by a 68-kilometre border, Denmark's only land frontier. Northwards, Danish Jutland tails away into a finger of land pointing towards Sweden, with its tip roughly on the same latitude as Gothenburg. The finger is called the Skaw, a great spit where picturesque lighthouses warn shipping against treacherous sandbanks. At its northernmost point, tourists may be photographed with one foot in the North Sea and the other in the Baltic.

To the north-west of the Skaw, Denmark is separated from Norway by a narrow channel called the Skagerrak. To the east, the sheltered approach to the islands between Jutland and Sweden is called the Kattegat.

Much of western Jutland looks pancake-flat, with expanses of broad, sandy heaths, spongy peat bogs, and empoldered marshes interspersed between well-tended farmland. Behind the North Sea beaches, the longest in Europe, is a rampart of sand dunes, driven eastwards by powerful western

21

1

winds and only prevented from engulfing farmlands by belts of protective conifers. In contrast, eastern Jutland has a hilly topography. Long inlets penetrate from the Kattegat, leading into steep-sided valleys where there are chains of lakes and woods of oak and beech. Further inland is Denmark's highest point, Yding Skovhøj (Yding Forest Mountain). But this "mountain" reaches a height of only 173 metres. As the Danish novelist, Martin A. Hansen, has written, Denmark is so lacking in high points offering extensive views that the smallness of the country is less apparent to the eye.

Despite its modest relief, the countryside of Jutland offers a landscape of many moods with its sturdy beech woods, its stiff plantations of pine, its patchwork of arable lands, lush-green meadows and purple summer heaths, its dyked marshlands and soft-flowing streams, its trim villages with neat, white-washed red-tiled farmhouses overlooking well-stocked gardens. Following reclamation of heathland and peat bogs in the 19th century, most of the land is in agricultural use. But the peninsula also has well-developed industries, especially in and around its principal port of Esbjerg on the west coast, the city of Aalborg in the north, and Aarhus, Denmark's second largest city, commonly called Jutland's capital, on the east coast.

South of Aarhus, at the once fortified town of Fredericia, two large bridges span the narrow strip of water, known as the Little Belt, which divides Jutland from the fertile island of Funen in the east. From these bridges, Funen—the so-called "Garden of Denmark"—is crossed by a major highway that leads to the port and university town of Odense (Hans Andersen's birthplace)

and on to the east coast, where car and train ferries regularly ply the Great Belt, dividing Funen from Zealand. Danes dream that one day a bridge will span this divide, so completing the road link between Jutland and Greater Copenhagen, the major metropolitan area that accommodates about a third of Denmark's population.

Copenhagen, capital of Denmark since 1443 and now Scandinavia's most populous city, derived its initial wealth from the abundance of herring in the Sound, the broad channel between the island of Zealand and south-west Sweden. With its free port, its ferry traffic, its shipyards and its overseas connections, it is still a "merchant's harbour", the origin of its Danish and Swedish name, the Øresund. Visually, it is reminiscent of Amsterdam. There is a strong Dutch influence in its Renaissance architecture, and it is a city that invites the pedestrian because of its profusion of courtyards, squares, public gardens, winding streets and alleyways. True, it lacks the canals of Amsterdam. Nevertheless, it subtly plays with water by way of the moats of former fortifications, ornamental pools and fountains, historic quays, and long sea-fronts, most notably the tree-lined Langelinje promenade, beside which the bronze Little Mermaid, inspired by a Hans Andersen fairy story, sits on a sea-washed rock amid a colourful array of private yachts.

But more than to Amsterdam, Copenhagen has been likened to the capital of France. In the language of the tourist brochures, it is "the Paris of the North", and though foreign visitors may find that description extravagant, by Nordic standards it is not without justification. No other city in Scandinavia has such a lively, free-and-easy at-

mosphere or such a vigorous night life. Copenhagen's most celebrated pleasure-grounds are the Tivoli Gardens, which boast a Chinese pagoda, Arabian-style "mosques", parading toy soldiers, a trapeze arena, side-shows and firework displays. The city's social life is less restricted by laws and conventions than elsewhere. There are more bars and restaurants per capita than in the other Scandinavian capitals; fewer restrictions on the sale of alcohol; and generally far greater scope for hedonistic pursuits.

In Copenhagen, the Danes can be seen at their most outgoing, recalling the English writer Evelyn Waugh's description of them as "the most exhilarating people in Europe". They are the *bons vivants* of the Nordic community: a warm and gregarious people who relish the wry prattle of their comedian Victor Borge and the witty poems of Piet Hein (Denmark's Ogden Nash). They are a people of hearty appetites, who submit to the temptations of glutinous cream pastries and the *smørrebrød*, the open Danish sandwich which balances a maximum of gustatory delights upon a minimum of rye bread. Also typically Danish are low-taxed cigars (commonly smoked by women as well as men), more than a hundred kinds of beer, "Peter Heering" cherry liqueur, and *akvavit*, a colourless spirit produced from potatoes or grain, and flavoured with caraway seeds.

Romantics tend to see Denmark in terms of its quainter images: Viking burial mounds on top of almost every hill and storks' nests on the chimney tops of farmhouses; white-washed medieval churches, grand castles and prim manor houses; chimney sweeps in traditional top hats and scarlet-uniformed postmen on yellow bicycles;

and the supremely popular Legoland Park, a Lilliputian realm created in Jutland by the Danish manufacturers of the toy building bricks. There is a certain quaintness, too, in the style of Denmark's ancient monarchy, which has taken to the common bicycle without rejecting such trappings of the imperial past as the Order of the Elephant (a decoration reserved for royalty and heads of state) and the busbied, red-tunicked soldiers who parade outside the magnificent, baroque Amalienborg Palace, the royal family's principal residence in central Copenhagen.

For the connoisseur, Denmark brings to mind the Royal Copenhagen porcelain and glittering Georg Jensen silverware, stylish furniture fashioned from imported tropical timbers, and a great range of high quality fabrics and household goods. (The Danes have achieved the ultimate in qualitative advertising far and wide by using just three words on their hoardings: "Good, Better, Danish".) More down-to-earth consumers are likely to identify Denmark with its remarkable output of agricultural products. It is the world's third largest exporter of cheese, the second largest exporter of butter, and the largest exporter of bacon. Indeed, in Denmark, pigs outnumber people by almost two to one, and each year they yield nearly 1 million tonnes of pork and bacon.

Yet despite this richness, only 7 per cent of the population engage in agriculture, fishing and forestry; the overwhelming majority of citizens live by industry, trade and service activities. And despite their taste for the good life, Danes are hard workers. Only thus is it possible to explain the extremely high standard of living achieved by a country naturally deficient in raw

THE COLD TABLE: AN ABUNDANCE OF CHOICE

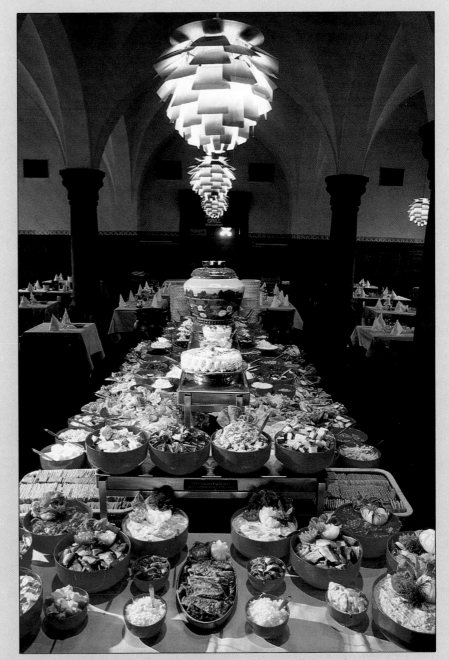

An array of cold dishes awaits patrons of Copenhagen's railway station restaurant.

The Danish equivalent of the Swedish and Finnish *smörgäsbord* is the *kolde bord*, literally "cold table". Prepared principally for lunches, its great diversity of dishes includes at least half a dozen varieties of pickled fish and as many spiced and smoked meats, accompanied by a selection of salads and pâtés, and sliced rye bread for making open sandwiches.

materials and, unlike Norway, Sweden, Finland and Iceland, almost completely without its own sources of energy.

Although a mere 130 kilometres of water separates the northern tip of Denmark from the southern coast of Norway, the contrast between the two countries could hardly be more dramatic. Whereas the landscape of Denmark is widely cultivated, well ordered and low-lying (Norwegians sometimes refer to the Danes as "Flatlanders"), the greater part of Norway is stark and rugged, almost primeval in aspect. Four fifths of its 324,219 square kilometres are at least 150 metres above sea level. It is one of the most mountainous countries in Europe—"Switzerland by the sea", as Honoré de Balzac described it. Physically, it is also one of the least developed Scandinavian countries, with less than 3 per cent of the land under cultivation.

Curving in a scenic arc of mountains, forests and fjords along the western side of Sweden, Norway has a shape which has been likened to that of a crouched lion, with its massive head and shoulders in the west, its forefeet in the south-east, and its long extended tail ending in a curl on the borders of the Soviet Union and Finland in the far north. With almost half of its length lying within the Arctic Circle, it can claim the world's most northerly town (Hammerfest) and the most northerly university (at Tromsø). Among other distinctions, it has Europe's deepest lake (500-metre deep Lake Hornindal) and largest mountain plateau (12,000-square kilometre Hardangervidda); the world's deepest fjord (1,308-metre Sognefjord), and several waterfalls far higher than Niagara.

But the most significant feature of this rugged, elongated land is its intimate relationship with the sea. Henrik Ibsen, Norway's supreme dramatist, once said that Norwegians were "hypnotized by water". This is no surprise, because about 75 per cent of its people live within sight of the coast. In addition, the country boasts numerous lakes, countless power-giving mountain rivers and waterfalls, and scores of fjords, including two—Sognefjord and Hardangerfjord—which penetrate as much as 130 kilometres inland. It is estimated that if all the fjords were straightened out, Norway's coastal span of 1,752 kilometres would be stretched to 20,112 kilometres, half the circumference of the earth.

Norway's name is born of the sea. It springs from a Norse word meaning "northern way", and refers to the 965-kilometre long sealane, sheltered by skerries and islands, which extends from Stavanger in the south-west to Tromsø in the north. For centuries, overland transport routes were so limited and hazardous that this offshore passage was the critical link between the widely scattered communities. Modern road, rail and air communications have lessened the importance of this seaway, but water is still a key influence on the life of the nation. Norway is a major shipping power. It also draws a rich harvest of fish from the sea, and gains an even richer harvest in the form of North Sea oil and gas.

Most significantly, water has revolutionized life in Norway by yielding an abundance of hydroelectric power. No country in the world has a greater wealth of water-driven energy in relation to its population. And this resource has greatly accelerated industrialization and urbanization. Less than a hundred years ago, most of the Norwegian working population derived a living from fishing, forestry and farming. Today, the figure is less than 10 per cent. The overwhelming majority of workers are now engaged in industry and service activities, and over 70 per cent of the population live in towns.

Norway is divided traditionally into five regions: lofty *Vestlandet* (Westland) in the south-west; wooded *Östlandet* (Eastland) in the south-east; sheltered *Sørlandet* (Southland), which extends along the Skagerrak coast; the more open land of the *Trøndelag* area in the centre; and *Nord-Norge* (Northern Norway), most of which lies north of the Arctic Circle. Following industrialization at the turn of the century, there has been a continuous drift of workers from the north to the cities of the south. More than half of Norway's 4.1 million population now lives in *Östlandet*, and the majority are concentrated in and around Oslo, the capital and the most important industrial, commercial and shipping centre.

The city of Oslo lies at the head of a 110-kilometre fjord opening on to the Skagerrak, thus giving sea access to Norway's principal trading partners—southern Sweden, Denmark, Germany, the Netherlands and Britain. The old fortress of Akershus overlooks the capital's deep-water harbour, which can accommodate cruise liners; and within shouting distance of Oslo's monumental town hall is a wharf where oil tankers of more than a quarter of a million tonnes have been built. The centre of the city is dominated by the neo-classical royal palace, built in the early

On the Danish island of Zealand, fields of yellow rape grown for animal feed and vegetable oil surround neat, white-washed farmhouses. With some 70 per cent of its land used for farming, Denmark is the most agricultural country in Scandinavia.

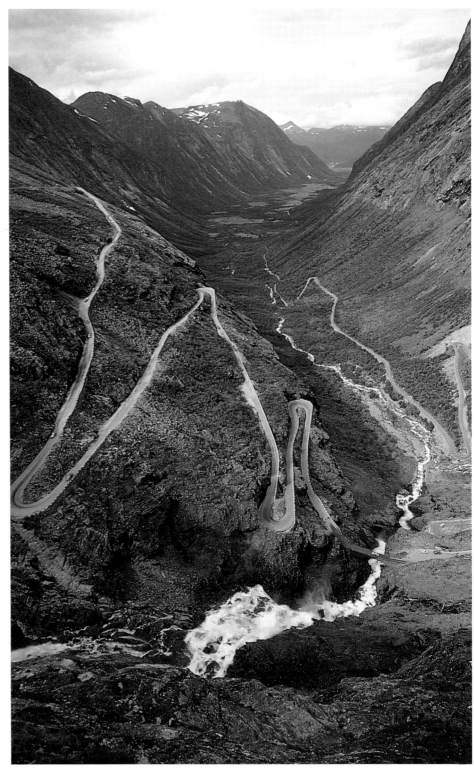

25

1

19th century and standing on high ground in a large, triangular-shaped park. Another park—far more famous (or infamous)—lies about two kilometres away. This is Frogner Park, for which the sculptor Gustav Vigeland spent more than three decades creating an elaborate arrangement of sculpture: hundreds of statues, mainly nudes, in all manner of shapes, sizes and postures. It is all on a staggering scale. Evelyn Waugh—no admirer of the sculptor's work—uncompromisingly described it as "a multitudinous subhuman zoo . . . far more awful than the ruins of Hiroshima".

In contrast to the more densely populated *Östlandet*, *Vestlandet* is the Norway of the travel brochures: leaping waterfalls, glaciers, innumerable offshore islands and skerries (Norwegians say they stopped counting at 50,000), and mountain flanks dropping in precipices to the sea, as if alpine peaks had been moved down to the coast and then sliced open with some gigantic cheesecutter. And in the far west, at Bergen—which is arguably Scandinavia's most picturesque city—the lofty works of nature blend supremely with the monuments of man.

Bergen was once the capital of Norway, and until 1800 was also the largest city. Now, although its population has been outpaced by that of Oslo, Bergen remains the cultural heart of *Vestlandet*, and is still distinguished by a style of its own. The Hanseatic harbour, filled with shipping and surrounded by a bustling open-air market, is backed by tiers of brightly painted weatherboard houses. The construction of a funicular railway, climbing to the top of Mount Floyen behind the town, has made more accessible the spectacular views that once inspired the Norwegian com-

poser Edvard Grieg, whose lakeside summer home, Troll Hill, stands on the outskirts of the city.

Vestlandet also takes in Norway's fourth largest city, Stavanger, a growing industrial centre with a fine peninsular setting. Since the opening of the North Sea fields at the beginning of the 1970s, this pleasant town of wooden, pantiled houses has become the nation's oil capital, a construction and supply base, and something of a goldrush settlement, accommodating an international community and immigrants from all over Norway.

Trøndelag is centred on the broad Trondheimfjord, where farm and forest country embrace Norway's third largest city, Trondheim, the seat of the archbishopric of Norway. Its Gothic-style cathedral is the burial-place of Norwegian kings. More significantly, as a major communications centre, Trondheim is at the fulcrum of Norway, so central that the Germans, during their occupation in World War II, planned to make it the national capital.

North Norway comprises the three counties of Nordland, Troms and Finnmark. The forest mantle is restricted to the sheltered dales, farming is limited, and the fisheries take precedence. Cod is the most valuable harvest—caught in vast quantities off the nearby Lofoten Islands in late winter and off the north coast in summer. The northernmost counties of Finnmark and Troms contain most of Norway's reindeer-herding Lapps, whose animals move by the thousand down to the coast for grazing in summer. Today, only a minority of Lapps move with them. Most are settled on smallholdings.

The largest towns in north Norway are Bodø on the Vestfjord; Mo i Rana, a major iron and steel producing

centre; Narvik, the iron ore terminal that was prominent during World War II operations; and Tromsø, a university town and the site of the Cathedral of the Arctic. Tromsø is also a traditional base for expeditions to the Arctic, and the terminal point for air and sea transport linking mainland Norway with Svalbard, the bleak archipelago some 640 kilometres to the north, which includes the island of Spitsbergen. In 1920, an international treaty accorded Norway sovereignty over the archipelago, and granted the 40 signatories of the treaty equal access to the islands for maritime, industrial, mining and commercial purposes. Today, some 2,000 Soviets take advantage of their treaty right, vying with about 1,000 Norwegians, who brave the island's harsh climate to mine half a million tonnes of coal a year.

The Norwegians, of course, are well accustomed to such challenging environments. The isolation imposed on them by mountains, wastes and forests, the imprisoning world of fjords and dales and long dark winters—these are factors that put a premium on self-reliance. Norway's heroes are men who stubbornly defy all odds in pursuit of their goals: men like Fridtjof Nansen, the polar explorer; Roald Amundsen, the first man to reach the South Pole; and the modern Viking, Thor Heyerdahl, who drifted for 101 days on the balsawood raft Kon-Tiki to corroborate a theory that Polynesia could have been settled by South Americans.

Living so close to an untamed, awesome environment has also invested many Norwegians with a keen sense of the supernatural. Generations of imaginative story-tellers have populated Norway with water sprites and witches, sea serpents and trolls. More

Two Lapp women in their traditional costume *(below)* lay out bundles of braid-trimming for sale at a Lapp festival in northern Finland. Male outfits are also richly embroidered, and feature an elaborate, silver-studded belt *(right)*.

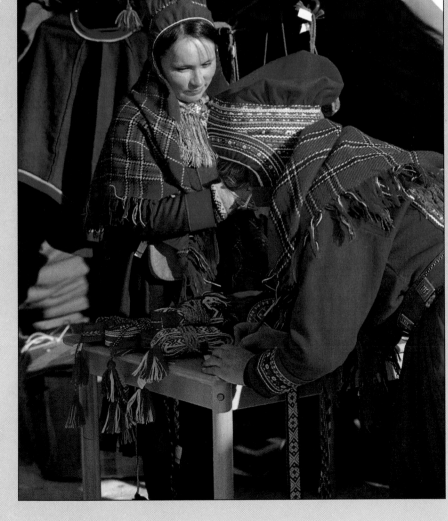

THE REINDEER HERDERS OF NORDIC LAPLAND

Across the Arctic and sub-Arctic areas of northern Norway, Sweden and Finland live an estimated 50,000 Lapps, an indigenous minority with a rich and distinctive cultural heritage. Known as *Sami* in their own language, the Lapps evolved a semi-nomadic lifestyle and survived for centuries by herding reindeer, fishing, hunting and trading in furs.

Today, the majority of Lapps are well integrated into Scandinavian society, but are increasingly assertive of their culture, their language and territorial rights. Only about 10 per cent continue to herd reindeer, helped by such modern conveniences as snowmobiles, two-way radios and even helicopters. The others are mainly settled on small farmsteads, where they eke out a modest living through casual labour. In addition, most families keep one or two cows, a few sheep and some domesticated reindeer, and cultivate a patch of land on which they grow potatoes and oats.

Outside a Lapp homestead in northern Norway, a snowmobile stands beside a trailer carrying a sledge, a more traditional Lapp conveyance once commonly drawn by reindeer. In the background, deerskins—eventually to be sold as rugs—hang out to dry on the walls of a wooden outhouse.

Lofty antlers provide an easy target for a young Lapp lassoing a reindeer in an annual roundup. There are more than half a million of the deer in Lapland, of which about a fifth are slaughtered yearly. Meat accounts for 90 per cent of an animal's cash value, with bone, horn and hide accounting for the rest.

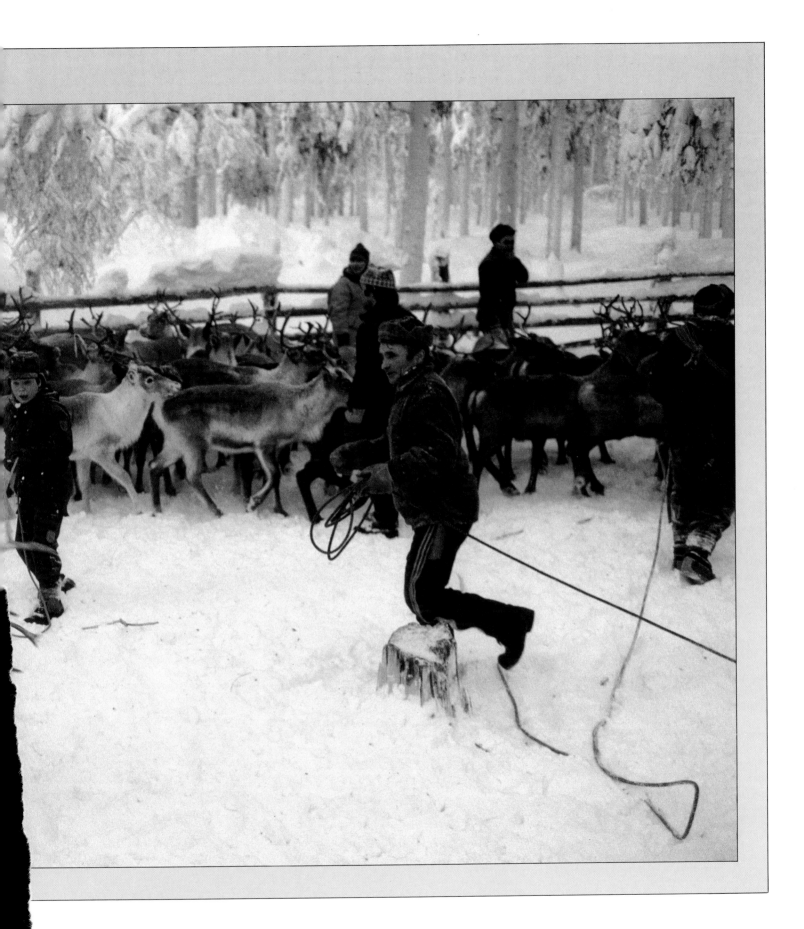

1

importantly, the magical atmosphere has been a powerful source of inspiration to novelists, painters, poets and composers, who have sought to capture the unique spirit of place that is manifest in so many parts of the country. When the 19th-century violinist Ole Bull, who enchanted European audiences with his performances of Norwegian folk melodies, was asked by the King of Denmark who had taught him to play, Bull simply replied: "The Norwegian mountains, your Majesty." The supreme statement of this Norwegian romanticism is Henrik Ibsen's *Peer Gynt*, which gathers together a whole tribe of supernatural creatures around a central character who is the apotheosis of individualism.

In general, the Norwegian people are fairly conservative in their outlook, with a strong streak of puritanism. There are no newspapers or alcohol on sale in Norway on the sabbath; and, significantly, the country was slower than its Danish and Swedish neighbours to accept legalized abortion and sex education. On the other hand, the people have a spontaneous sense of fun and a great love of sport. As visiting foreigners have often observed, most Norwegians seem to have achieved a high standard of living without becoming slaves to materialism and without losing sight of human values.

Like all the Scandinavian countries, Norway is a parliamentary democracy, with the legislative power vested in the 150-strong *Storting* (Parliament). The king is a figurehead, taking no part in political issues. In modern times, all the royal children have married commoners—unsurprisingly, since there have been no titled families other than royalty in Norway since 1821, when the parliament voted to abolish nobility.

Many years later, Ibsen remarked that "Norwegians can only agree on one point—to drag down the lofty". The result has been the most egalitarian society in mainland Europe.

Although it shares with Norway a 1,619-kilometre long border, Sweden has rather more in common physically with its other immediate neighbour, Finland, which it faces across the brackish Gulf of Bothnia in the east and across a 586-kilometre land frontier in the north. To be sure, it sometimes recalls Norway's scenic magnificence, with deep valleys, great waterfalls, and mountain peaks as much as 2,000 metres high in Swedish Lapland. For the greater part, however, Sweden is relatively low-lying and, like Finland, it has myriad lakes and rivers, and vast coniferous forests.

This is the largest country in Scandinavia, and the fourth largest in Europe. Its varied landscapes, ranging from modest glaciers in the far north to sandy beaches in the south-west, are largely explained by the fact that it extends some 1,574 kilometres latitudinally. In its south-west province of Skåne—rich farmland with broad open fields of autumn grain, glossy-leafed sugar beet and other arable crops—Sweden also shares topographical characteristics with Denmark. It is popularly said by Swedes that God gave Skåne to Sweden to show them what Europe looks like.

Perhaps the most distinctive feature of Sweden is the fact that almost all settlement is water-orientated, either coastal, lakeside or riverside. An impressive series of parallel rivers cross the northern half of the country diagonally, disgorging through waterfalls and rapids from the mountain lakes on the Norwegian border to the shallow estuaries on the Bothnian Sea. And lakes of all sizes—at least 90,000 of them—are scattered throughout the land. Some are so large that the early inhabitants regarded them as inland seas. They include the third largest lake in Europe, the 5,546-square kilometre Lake Vänern, which is linked to the west coast city of Gothenburg by the Göta canal.

This marriage of land and water is further emphasized by the infinitely fragmented character of the generally low-lying Swedish coasts. They are rich in archipelagos, some of them of extraordinary complexity. For example, the hundreds of wooded islands at the approaches to Stockholm provide a veritable maze of waterside escapes for the Swedish people to enjoy in summer. Contrastingly, there are innumerable wave-swept, granite islands in the exposed archipelago of the western region of Bohuslän.

Sweden also has two islands of notable size. Off the south-east coast, the long, narrow limestone island of Öland is linked to the historic mainland city of Kalmar by a magnificent bridge, 6,060 metres long and with more than 150 piers. Beyond it, in mid-Baltic, lies Sweden's largest island, Gotland, with its fabled, walled capital of Visby, the most impressive medieval town in all Scandinavia. Once a Viking stronghold and later Sweden's richest trading centre, Gotland is now mainly a farming community, and such a popular tourist resort that in summer visitors outnumber the island population of 54,000 by about four to one.

On the mainland, trees rival lakes and rivers as the dominant feature of the Swedish countryside. There were 51 billion of them at the last estimate,

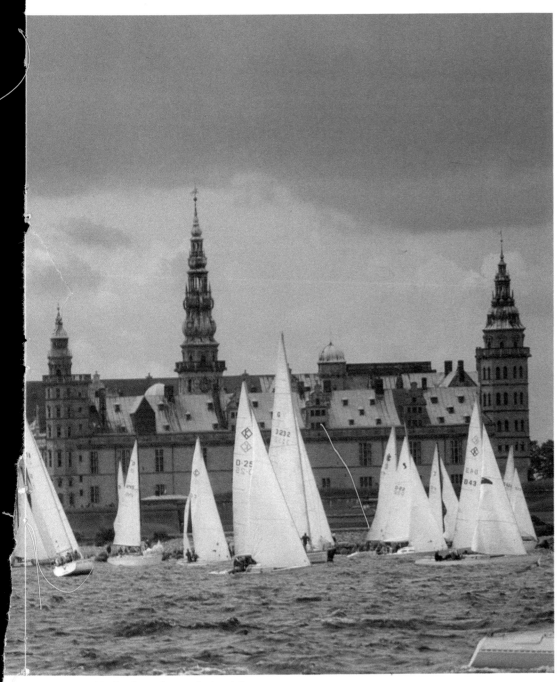

Yachts from the nearby Danish port of Helsingør sweep past Kronborg Castle, a Renaissance stronghold overlooking the choppy Øresund. For over 400 years, until 1857, tolls were levied on all foreign ships passing through the channel, at its narrowest here, just 5 kilometres from Sweden.

1

varying from white-barked birch and dark green pine and spruce in the north to beech and oak woods in the southwest. Sweden boasts the largest softwood timber reserves in all of Europe, and, together with Finland, its woodlands—covering more than half the nation's land area—are more carefully managed than those of any other country in the world.

Being relatively rich in mineral resources—especially iron and other basic ores—Sweden has always been the most industrialized of the Nordic countries. It is also the most urbanized. About 90 per cent of the population of 8.3 million now live in the southern half of the country, the greatest concentrations being in the major metropolitan areas of Stockholm, Gothenburg and Malmö. Of these, Stockholm is by far the largest, with more than 1.5 million residents. It is also more centrally located in relation to its country than any other Nordic capital.

Stockholm (the name means a stockaded island, or holm) was founded in the 13th century at the narrows where Lake Mälar meets the Baltic Sea. The city is so interlaced with waterways that it has, inevitably, been called "the Venice of the North"; and though the title is a little ambitious it is at least supported by many spires and domes, old and new, by a wealth of baroque architecture, by an attractive neo-

A passenger ferry sails past several of the 24,000 or more islands in the Baltic that constitute the Stockholm archipelago. Romantically named the *Skärgård*, or Garden of Skerries, these islands are peppered with thousands of summer homes occupied by Swedes at weekends and for vacations.

romantic city hall, and by the city's many bridges and waterside walks and piazzas. Much of the Old Town of Stockholm, having escaped both war and fires, is intact, with its original marketplace and a maze of narrow cobbled streets lined with gabled buildings, many of which now house antique shops. The trappings of monarchy still exist in its renaissance-style royal palace. In the chapels of the city's medieval Riddarholm church, once part of a monastery, are the tombstones of every Swedish monarch since 1632 with the exception of Queen Christina, who was converted to Roman Catholicism and eventually buried in Rome.

Apart from its archipelago and its waterways, the greatest recreational assets in Stockholm are its parks and open spaces. Kungstradgården, the Royal Garden close by the palace, is the most centrally located. To the east are Ladugården and Djurgården (Deer Park). The latter was a royal hunting preserve from the 16th to the 18th century, but it is now most renowned as the site of Scandinavia's oldest and largest open-air museum, Skansen. Designed to preserve examples of life in pre-industrial Sweden, Skansen contains scores of historic buildings that have been transplanted from various parts of the country. They include a church and a manor house, Lapp dwellings, peasant farmhouses, and workshops in which old crafts such as butter and cheese making, weaving, wood-turning and glass-blowing are demonstrated. In addition, Skansen has a zoo, restaurants and a summer theatre.

On the west coast, four hours by train from Stockholm, is Gothenburg, Sweden's largest seaport and second largest city. In this breezy metropolis, the atmosphere is noticeably different:

In the Vasastan district of central Stockholm, apartment blocks constructed at the turn of the century stretch out like ticker-tape in the sun. The blocks, which house mainly middle-class families, are built around two, or sometimes even three, courtyards.

more extrovert and vigorous, reflecting its North Sea outlook. Some 40 per cent of Sweden's merchant fleet is harboured at Gothenburg. From the lofty suspension bridge that spans its busy Göta River may be seen the impressive factories that produce Volvo vehicles, Mölnlycke textiles, and the steel products of SKF, one of the world's leading producers of ball-bearings.

The citizens of Gothenburg regard themselves as being essentially independent of their far-off capital in the east. Malmö, Sweden's third largest city in the extreme south, is even further from Stockholm. It is linked to the Copenhagen area by a constant shuttle of ferries and hydrofoils across the Sound, so its citizens have a closer association with the Danish capital than with Stockholm. Nevertheless, a recognizably similar lifestyle unites most of the inhabitants of the nation's populous southern provinces. Indeed, in all of Sweden's leading cities, most people live in well-designed, ultra-modern high-rise apartment blocks. Yet whenever possible, they will escape to the countryside, often staying in pri-

mitive wooden dwellings without plumbing and far away from public services. The yearning for the great outdoors is partly compensatory, because Sweden is one of the most developed countries in the world. Affluence is manifest everywhere. Sweden is near the top of international league tables for the possession of cars, televisions, refrigerators and telephones; and the nation's gross national product is rivalled only by Switzerland and Norway among European countries.

Sweden's prosperity is the product of a mixed economy. Long ago, the nation developed a social order described as "the middle way" between capitalism and socialism. Some economic sectors—for example, railways, post offices and telecommunications—are state-owned, but about 90 per cent of Swedish industry is in private hands. At the same time, the co-operative movement thrives on a far greater scale than in most other European countries, and about 80 per cent of the work force belong to a trade union.

Although the left-of-centre Social Democratic party was in power almost

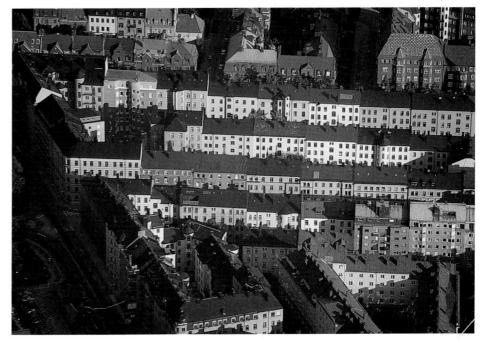

HELSINKI'S BUSTLING WATERSIDE MARKET

A colourful feature of Helsinki life is the open-air market on the spacious waterfront of the South Harbour. It operates from 7 a.m. to 2 p.m. every Monday to Saturday, except in mid-winter. When the waterways are clear of ice, Finns from outlying islands tie up their boats along the quay and sell a wide range of home-grown produce as well as salmon, whitefish, herring and crayfish. In addition, waterside stalls offer freshly cut flowers and potted plants for sale, along with such household goods as brooms, baskets, rag carpets, and that indispensable feature of the Finnish sauna, the birch whisk.

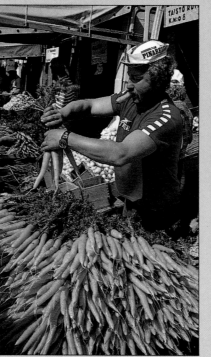

A man sells carrots from a market stall.

Smoked herrings are displayed on a boat.

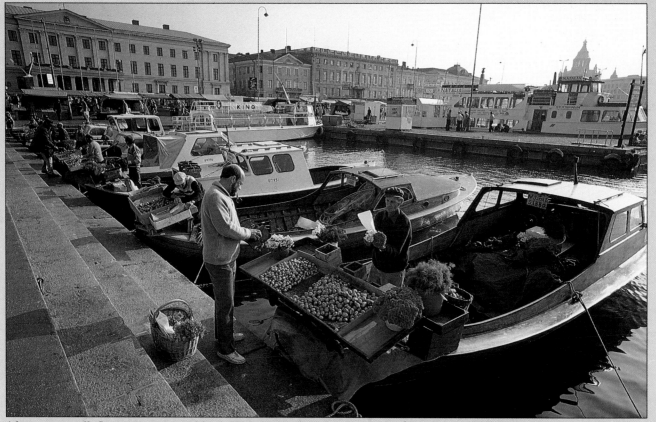

A boat-owner sells flowers, potatoes and fresh dill from the stern of his launch. In the background, stalls crowd the harbour-side.

continuously from 1932 to 1976, it never made a fetish of nationalization. By the same token, industrial and trade policy did not undergo any fundamental change after 1976 when a non-socialist coalition Cabinet was formed. Swedish governments have avoided extreme political stances. Instead, they have concentrated, with a large measure of success, on promoting economic growth and sustaining as far as possible a well-established system of social welfare—the most advanced of its kind in the world.

To an even greater degree than neighbouring Sweden, Finland is a country of woodland and water. On a large-scale map, it looks rather like a jigsaw puzzle two thirds completed on a table of blue. The gaps are lakes—some 62,000 of them, ranging from lonely forest pools visited only by elk and crane to great sheets of inland water such as Saimaa, the fifth largest lake in Europe. To pursue the simile, the unused pieces scattered around the jigsaw puzzle would be Finland's tens of thousands of offshore islands and islets, of which some 7,000 constitute the Åland archipelago, an autonomous province that is situated midway between Finland and Sweden.

In summer, the dominant colour of this fragmented country is green—not the bright acid green of cultivated land, which comprises less than 10 per cent of Finland's 337,032 square kilometres, but the dark, boreal hues of pine and spruce forests which spread over nearly 70 per cent of the territory. This is Europe's most forested country. Only above the Arctic Circle do the trees begin to peter out, to be replaced by great tracts of moor, bogland and fell dotted with lichen-covered outcrops of the granite shield that underlies the thin soil. Almost everywhere else, the forest closes in, tranquil and melancholy, hypnotic and monotonous, blanketing the low ridges and hills.

In the treeless north-west there are mountains a thousand metres high, but in many other areas of Finland the only way to see the wood from the trees is to climb the high ridges of sand and gravel, which snake like eccentric railway embankments over the landscape. Called eskers, these ridges were deposited by the ice sheet that buried Finland 10,000 years ago. At the same time, the ice created myriad lakes by scouring hollows in the land. Finland has still not recovered from the ice age—literally, since in some areas the land is rising from the sea at the rate of nearly 80 centimetres a century as it regains its geological equilibrium after shedding its glacial burden.

Geographically, this is one of the northernmost countries in the world, with approximately one third of its land within the Arctic Circle. In the north, the first snows often fall in late September, blizzards may strike well into May, and mean temperatures are likely to remain below −5°C for 160 days or more. The rigorous climate helps to explain why a country about 40 per cent larger than Britain has only 4.8 million inhabitants, compared with 56 million in Britain. More precisely, it indicates why two thirds of the Finnish population is settled in the southern third of the country. There, in urban municipalities, the population density is 81 inhabitants per square kilometre, whereas in Lappi, the largest and most northern of Finland's 12 provinces, it is only 1.2 people per square kilometre.

Almost one million Finns—a fifth of the population—live in Helsinki's metropolitan area. Another quarter of a million live in and around the city of Turku, the capital until 1812 and still the ecclesiastical centre of the Evangelical Lutheran Church, to which more than 90 per cent of the population belongs. Tampere, a thriving industrial centre 170 kilometres north-west of Helsinki, is Finland's other big city; the rest of the urban population—60 per cent of the total—live in towns with fewer than 90,000 inhabitants.

Less than 15 per cent of the population is now engaged in farming and forestry, as opposed to some 50 per cent in 1950. However, despite a steady drift from villages to towns, Finland is not as intensively urbanized as most other industrialized countries. There are still many small industrial communities, and even the loneliest traveller is likely at some time to catch sight of the chimney of an isolated paper mill, or see a great raft of tree trunks on a lake, at the start of a journey to the timber mills and workshops that produce more than a third of the nation's export earnings.

In Finland, as in Sweden and Norway, almost all towns have a waterside setting which, together with their spacious layouts and generous areas of parkland, makes them appear large in proportion to their populations. This is even true of Helsinki, the cultural and commercial heart of the country. Helsinki is Finland's largest industrial city and its busiest port, a capital whose wealth of monumental buildings are concentrated in the neo-classical core surrounded by high-rise residential districts. Its many parks, broad boulevards and seafront promenades give the city an air of spaciousness. Even so, there is never quite space enough for the country-loving Finn. Like Sweden's capital, Helsinki tends to empty in summertime, especially at weekends, as tens of thousands of city dwellers make an exodus to waterside cottages and forest cabins, all of which have their own sauna, virtually a place of worship for the overwhelming majority of the population.

It is a migration pattern common to all of Finland. Whenever possible, the people like to escape the urban areas—in summer, to boat, fish, swim or pick berries; in autumn, to gather mushrooms, to hunt elk or deer; in winter, to take to their skis. As a native of Helsinki expresses it, "Scratch a Finn and you find an animist. We want to go into the forest, to be alone and have a private dialogue with nature."

Such a yearning for solitude constitutes something of a paradox. As individuals, living in such a spacious, tranquil land, the Finns seek their own remote, isolated worlds. As a nation, however, they have always been haunted by a sense of isolation. This is largely the result of history and geography. Unlike the Danes, Norwegians and Swedes, the Finns took little or no part in the far-ranging Viking explorations of a thousand years ago. For more than 600 years, from the 12th century until 1809, Finland was part of Sweden and often served as a buffer to Russian aggression. It then became a Grand Duchy of Russia until gaining independence in 1917. As European tourism developed, foreigners increasingly travelled to Denmark, Norway and Sweden, but Finland lay off the tourists' track until more recent years.

More particularly, the Finnish sense of isolation has been fostered by a language that is unrelated to any Norse tongue or to Russian. Finnish, like Estonian and Lappish, belongs to the so-called Finno-Ugrian family of languages, which supports the theory that the Finns are descendants of peoples who had their origin near the Ural Mountains and moved westwards in a series of migrations starting about 4,000 years ago. Because of the language barrier, the nation has suffered from a degree of cultural isolation. To be sure, some achievements have transcended the barrier. Through music—most notably that of Sibelius—Finland has found a universal tongue, while through the works of Alvar Aalto and other outstanding architects, Finland has acquired designs for living that have been adopted by many countries. But its considerable literary achievement has gone largely unrecognized. Apart from translations of the great Finnish folk epic *Kalevala*, Finnish literature remains a closed book to most of the world.

One way in which the sense of isolation manifests itself today is in an obsessive concern about the overseas image of Finland and its people. As Erkki Toivanen, the Paris correspondent of the Finnish Broadcasting Company, explained: "Finns are obsessed about the knowledge, or lack of it, others have of our country. Now that what used to be Europe is divided into 'Europe', Soviet bloc, and Scandinavia, we are desperately trying to impress the Scandinavishness of Finland on foreigners. It is of vital importance to our self-esteem that people know where we live, who we are ruled by, and under what kind of system."

Finland's institutions are Western European. Its educational system follows the German model; its rural co-operative structures have been inspired by those of Denmark; its legal, administrative and constitutional systems are cast in the Swedish mould. And this parliamentary republic is headed by a democratically elected president whose powers are largely based upon those of the American presidency.

However, for all their Western-style institutions, the Finns cannot afford to ignore the necessity of maintaining a respectful relationship with the Soviets. Only China and Mongolia have a longer frontier with the Soviet Union. Over the centuries, Finland has fought

In the hotel at Mundal, a Norwegian village nestling on an arm of the Sognefjord, guests at a wedding reception drink a toast to the bride and groom. Most of the women wear folk costume, a tradition still widespread on festive occasions.

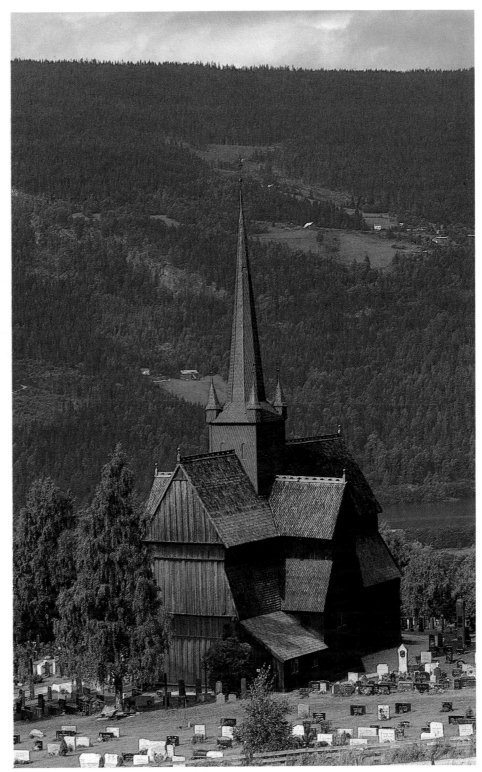

numerous wars against the Russians and lost every one of them. The last bitter conflict, from 1941 to 1944, cost the Finns 10 per cent of their land, including the country's only outlet to the Arctic Sea, and 300 million dollars' worth of reparations. Recently, it has been estimated that Finland's military establishment—strictly organized on defensive lines—is one three-hundredth the size of its Soviet neighbour's. And it is a sobering thought that in the city of Leningrad alone— just 150 kilometres over the border— there are more Soviet citizens than there are Finns in the whole of Finland.

It is little wonder then that the 1948 Soviet-Finnish Treaty of Friendship, Co-operation and Mutual Assistance has been twice extended (now until the year 2003) and that Finnish leaders consistently eschew criticism of Soviet politics. Finland endeavours to maintain a strict neutrality in its east-west affairs, and to give equal attention to fostering good relations with both capitalist and communist countries. By and large, it has managed to sustain its goodwill double-act with a high degree of success. Its diplomatic dexterity is exemplified by its purchase of armaments: it buys one third of its defence weaponry from the Soviet Union, one third from the West, and one third from either neutral countries or its own arms industries.

Finland has also contrived to turn its dual relationships to economic advantage. By means of a series of five-year agreements, it has provided the Soviet Union—its biggest single trading partner—with ships and industrial goods in exchange for oil and natural gas. At the same time, Finland has developed strong economic links with the West through the Nordic Council, the Organization for Economic Co-operation and Development (OECD), EFTA and free trade agreements with the EEC. This unique trading position helped Finland to weather the world recession in the 1970s. Indeed, by the mid-1980s, Finland was showing the fastest growth rate among members of the OECD, even surpassing that of Japan.

Attempting to explain to Westerners the pragmatic nature of their country's neutrality, Finnish officials sometimes relate an old anecdote dating from the civil war of 1918, when Red Guards (pro-Bolshevik Finns aided by Russian revolutionaries) were ranged against White Guards (anti-Bolshevik Finns aided by German troops). A man is standing on the Tampere bridge after dark when he suddenly feels the barrel of a soldier's rifle pressed in the small of his back. "Red or white?" the soldier demands. "May I first know who is asking?" inquires the civilian.

The Finns face up to their position on the tightrope between East and West with fortitude. The quality they most admire is *sisu*—a composite word meaning courage, resilience, the refusal to accept defeat. *Sisu* has made the Finns eminent in the more gruelling forms of sporting competition such as long-distance running and skiing, and marathon car rallies. It is the quality that has contributed above all others to Finland's emergence and survival as an independent nation.

Unlike the Finns, or indeed any of their Nordic partners, the people of Iceland have never experienced war directly. Yet, in their own way, they also deserve to be characterized in terms of *sisu*, having contended with forces of an especially awesome kind. For centuries, the Icelanders had to

A boy in Oslo, jokingly dressed in an outsize jacket and top hat, clutches a flag as he joins in celebrations of Norway's national day. Each year, on May 17, the anniversary of the Constitution of 1814 is marked by processions and ceremonies on a scale unequalled in Scandinavia.

struggle for survival on a remote island constantly ravaged by volcanic eruptions, earthquakes, famine and disease. Their country remains the most volcanically active land in Europe, and it is still subject to earthquakes.

A vivid reminder of Iceland's violent history came on the morning of November 14, 1963, when the crew of an Icelandic fishing boat sighted a huge column of black smoke rising far out to sea. Presuming a ship to be in distress, they raced to the rescue. Instead, they found a position—some 27 kilometres off the south-west coast of Iceland— where the sea had become a boiling cauldron from which billowed great clouds of ash and vapour. The following day, a black cone of lava rose some 10 metres above the seething waters, and sent lumps of red-hot rock flying into the steam-filled air. For more than

two years, volcanic eruptions continued, in the process creating an island nearly 2.8 square kilometres in size. Icelanders called their new offshore territory "Surtsey", after Surtur, the fire-making giant of Norse legend.

With such spectacle and fury, on an infinitely larger scale and over millions of years, Iceland itself was created— born of fire out of water. In the course of countless eruptions, it has grown to its present-day size of 103,000 square kilometres, making it, after Greenland and Britain, the third largest island in Europe. Historically, it is one of the older nations of the world; yet it also remains one of the smallest, with a mere 237,000 inhabitants.

This land of legends is believed to have been first settled by Irish monks in the eighth century. However, according to *Landnambok*, the nation's historic *"Book of Settlements"*, compiled in the 13th century, the Norwegian chieftain Ingolfur Arnarson was the first permanent settler in the year 874. The story claims that, when in sight of land, he threw the wooden pillars of his ancestral Norwegian home into the sea, vowing that he would settle where they came ashore. Three years later, he found the pillars in a little bay which he named Reykjavik ("Bay of Smoke"). Whatever the historical accuracy of the tale, it has always been dear to the Icelanders, who have seen the hidden hand of fate in Reykjavik's emergence as Iceland's capital and principal centre of population.

An earlier Viking explorer, Floki Vigerdarson, is credited with having disparagingly coined the name "Iceland", after judging the land unfit for human habitation. It was a misleading choice. About 11.65 per cent of the island's surface is covered by glaciers,

Three of the guards assigned to the
royal palace in central Oslo relax
outside the adjoining guardhouse
before going on duty. The ceremonial
uniforms are the star attraction of
the changing of the guard ceremony,
which takes place in front of the
palace at 1.30 p.m. daily.

and Vatnajökull, 8,400 square kilometres, is the largest glacier in Europe;
but ice is by no means the dominant
characteristic. A far more accurate title
would have been "Lavaland", for basal-
tic rocks and solidified lava cooled and
eroded into weird shapes, provide
much of the island's fantastic scenery.

Altogether, Iceland has some 200
volcanoes known to have been active in
post-glacial times. Of these, more than
20 are still active, the most celebrated
being Mount Hekla, once so fiery that
medieval writers identified it as one of
the main gates to hell. Contrastingly,
the most beautiful of all the volcanic
peaks is Snaefell, whose Fujiyama-like
profile can be seen on a clear day in
Reykjavik, almost hanging in the air
some 110 kilometres away across Faxa-
floi Bay. It was down the throat of
Snaefell that Jules Verne's fictional
heroes made their journey to the centre
of the earth.

An eruption of some kind occurs in
this country roughly once every five
years. The last time volcanic activity
caused serious damage was in January
1973, when the entire 5,300-plus population of Heimaey, the only inhabited
island in Iceland's offshore Westman
group, had to be evacuated within a
few hours of the first rumble. The eruption lasted for more than three months
and left the island's only town, Vest-
mannaeyjar, half-submerged in lava
and half-buried in ashes.

As a result of centuries of eruptions,
much of Iceland has a bald, open appearance, being so naked of trees that
even modest areas of birch scrub are
graced with the name of woodland.
The scenery in the vast, uninhabited
interior conjures up images of lunar
landscapes; indeed, in the mid-1960s,
American astronauts were flown there

Icelandic shepherds on horseback herd a flock of sheep to pasture. Sheep were introduced to Iceland by Norse settlers 11 centuries ago. Now, about 750,000 are bred for their meat, wool and skins—traditionally Iceland's second main source of income, after fishing.

so that they could familiarize themselves with the kind of terrain likely to be encountered on the moon. Mainly, this terrain comprises extensive ash-deserts, some of them relics of the great eruption of 1783 that destroyed thousands of animals, poisoned vegetation and grazing lands, created a famine that ultimately caused the deaths of about 25,000 people and, at its peak, shot dust so high into the atmosphere that the effects were recorded by Benjamin Franklin, who was 2,000 kilometres away in Paris.

Everywhere there are constant reminders of the massive natural power that lies beneath the earth's surface. They take the form of bubbling mud pools, hundreds of hot springs, and, most spectacularly, the famous Great Geysir, from which the English word "geyser" derives. Hot springs provide central heating for 80 per cent of all houses in Iceland, supply warm water for nearly 30 open-air bathing pools, and sustain tropical greenhouses in which tomatoes, grapes, melons, pineapples, bananas and even coffee beans are grown.

Inevitably, this harsh and rugged land has forged a tough and resilient people. Its isolation—the nearest neighbour is Scotland, some 750 kilometres away—has also been a significant influence. Left to their own devices, far removed from the mainstream of European development, the Icelanders have forged a remarkably homogeneous and egalitarian society, undivided by variations in race, creed or tongue. The language has changed relatively little in structure or sound from that of the ninth-century settlers, and Icelanders claim that it is the oldest in common everyday use in the world. This tradition is so cherished that leading acade-

Box-like houses with corrugated roofs of many different colours surround Lake Tjornin in the heart of Reykjavik, the capital city of Iceland. Reykjavik and nearby settlements accommodate some 120,000 people, more than 50 per cent of Iceland's total population.

mics search for obsolete words that may be revived with new meanings. For example, *simi* ("long thread") is now used to mean a telephone.

Iceland's remoteness was effectively ended by the opening of regular air passenger services after World War II. In 1950, the country was visited by 5,000 foreigners; by the mid-1980s, the number of tourists had increased more than tenfold. Iceland was also drawn more and more into the international arena as a member of the United Nations, EFTA, OECD, the Council of Europe, NATO and the Nordic Council. Meanwhile, in the wake of industrialization, Icelanders have become much less isolated within their own country. In the two decades following World War II, the country was transformed from an essentially rural and agricultural society into an urbanized society with an industrial economy. Today, almost two thirds of the people live in or near Reykjavik in the climatically favoured south-west, and manufacturing and services now employ the greater part of the working population.

Nevertheless, fishing remains critical to the economic life of Iceland, and

accounts for about 75 per cent of all exports. Only about 1 per cent of the land is cultivated. The climate restricts crops to grass, oats and potatoes. Accordingly, animal husbandry takes absolute pride of place in agriculture, to the extent that Iceland is self-sufficient in meat, poultry and dairy products. Sheep, above all, dominate the rural scene—more than three quarters of a million of them, kept out of the infields by Iceland's ubiquitous fencing material, barbed wire. They are herded on the grazing lands with the aid of the island's distinctive ponies, which are hardy enough to withstand the inclement climate, sure-footed enough to cover the rough countryside, and so small that they are measured in thumbs instead of hands.

Although the majority of Icelanders now live in a modern, urbanized society, they remain doggedly traditional and conservative, jealously guarding their culture and ever wary of foreign influence. The existence of a big American NATO base at Keflavik, 48 kilometres west of the capital, has been a subject of controversy ever since it was established in 1951. It has provided a valuable boost to the national economy, and yet, in 1980, Iceland's newly elected first woman president, Vigdis Finnbogadottir, described the base as "an unpleasant necessity". By the same token, Iceland's state-owned radio and television are on guard against foreign words that might creep into common usage and dilute the purity of the Icelandic language. Warnings against such intrusions are frequently broadcast. More positively, there are weekly readings on radio of Sagas and Eddas, the old stories extolling the virtues of Iceland's early settlers, and the brave deeds of ancient heroes and gods.

But while Icelanders have won a reputation for being the most fiercely independent and conservative of Scandinavians, they are also, paradoxically, the most enthusiastic members of the Nordic community. An opinion poll commissioned by the Nordic Council in 1983 revealed that Iceland valued Nordic co-operation far more highly than any other Scandinavian country. Unlike Icelanders, the Danes, Finns, Norwegians and Swedes tended to express special interest in individual Nordic countries. However, a majority of people in all five countries were in total agreement about one point: Nordic unity should always take precedence over European links.

In many ways, the Scandinavian countries today co-operate far more in-

timately than any other similar union of independent states. Nevertheless, Scandinavia is more aptly described as a family of nations rather than a federation of states. As Patricia Bliss McFate, president of the American Scandinavian Foundation, has observed: "One sometimes hears the phrase 'Nordic family'. The analogy is helpful not because one can try to pick out the big brother and the naughty little sister, but because it suggests kinship. The countries are a family that grew up together, sharing experiences and beliefs. Now they live apart, but they are siblings. And, although they tease one another, and occasionally quarrel bitterly, they won't fight."

A LAND OF AWESOME POWER AND INFINITE ENERGY

Iceland is the largest volcanic island in the world, a 103,000-square-kilometre landmass sitting astride deep fractures in the earth's crust. Most of the geothermal activity occurs in a belt stretching across the island from north-east to south-west. The country's primeval landscape is dramatically scarred with active, snow-capped volcanoes, spouting geysers, hot-water springs, bubbling mud pots and fumaroles (vents emitting hot steam). All testify to the continuing molten ferment deep below Iceland's basalt bedrock.

These forces are now being harnessed to provide one third of Iceland's energy demands. In the capital, Reykjavik, hot water is drawn directly from under the city itself, as well as from neighbouring districts, and then stored in huge tanks before being piped to the home radiators of 97 per cent of the city's population. For consumers, the use of local energy rather than expensive imported fuel has resulted in savings of up to 25 per cent on heating bills. Besides warming homes, subterranean hot water also fills about 30 year-round open-air swimming pools, supplies the breeding tanks of fish hatcheries, and heats the country's greenhouses—now covering a total of 150,000 square metres—in which are produced fruit, vegetables and flowers.

Such are the benefits of Iceland's immense natural power. At the same time, Icelanders are acutely aware of its destructive potential. On average, every decade brings two bouts of volcanic activity. The most dramatic of recent eruptions came in 1973 when a volcano on the island of Heimaey, 12 kilometres off the south coast of Iceland, destroyed much of the island's only town and forced the evacuation of over 5,000 people to the mainland. They returned soon after to rebuild their homes and their lives, but the volcano remains a threat.

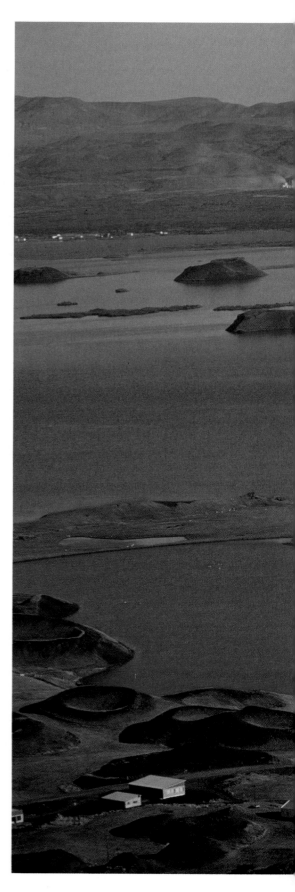

Sunlight catches a small settlement on the shores of Lake Mývatn in northeast Iceland. The peace of the scene is belied by the nature of the landscape, incorporating lava terrain, volcanic stumps rising from the water and steam escaping from a field of hot springs beside the distant hills.

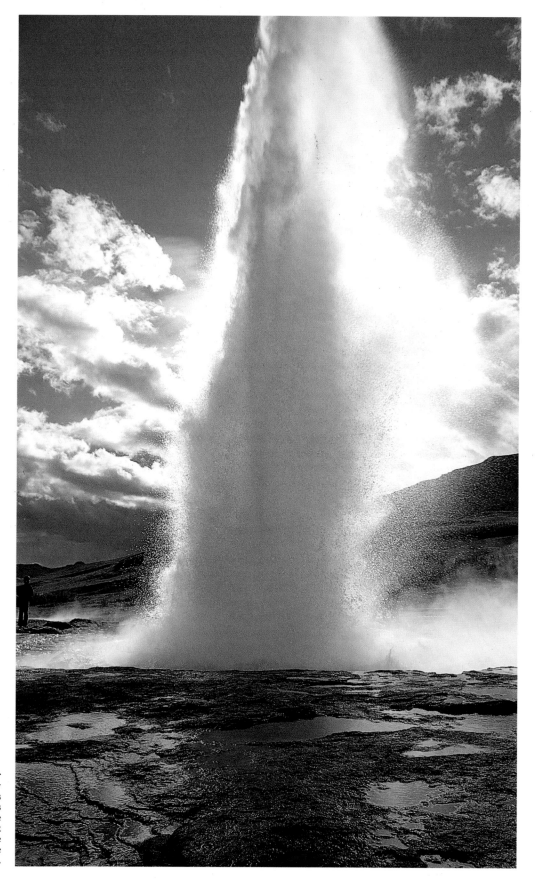

During one of its spectacular eruptions—which occur roughly every 10 minutes—the geyser known as Strokkur (literally, "the Churn") hurls hot water and steam 10 metres into the air. Situated 80 kilometres north-east of Reykjavik, the spout bursts into life when superheated water comes to the boil and is blasted out of the earth.

ERUPTIONS FROM SUBTERRANEAN FURNACES

Subterranean steam blows bubbles in a mud pot at Námaskard.

Steam rises from a fumarole at Hveravellir, north of Námaskard.

Shallow terraces formed by successive eruptions of muddy water encircle another steam hole at Hveravellir.

HARNESSING THE FORCES OF NATURE

A pipeline carrying water to cool the drills of the experimental Krafla geothermal power station snakes across a laval landscape in north-east Iceland. In the background, steam from the station's drillholes, which tap into subterranean hot springs, rises in a thick cloud.

Clouds of steam rise from chimneys of the Sudurnes geothermal plant at Svartsengi in south-west Iceland. The plant is the first in the world to generate power from high-temperature brine, through a complex process in which the energy-producing hot steam is separated from the unusably saline water, which is discarded.

Less than 2 kilometres from the Lutheran church on Heimaey Island, a colossal pillar of smoke and ash rises upwards from a fissure formed overnight by volcanic action. The outflow of molten lava created a hill 275 metres high.

In the aftermath of the eruption, the surviving houses stand engulfed in a 4-metre deep blanket of black tephra—the fragments of volcanic ash, cinders and pumice ejected in the blow-out. Beyond, steam rises off the volcano's still-warm lava fields.

A VOLCANO'S DESTRUCTIVE TRACK

Gustavus II Adolphus, commanding a
13,000-strong Swedish army, kneels in
prayer before his invasion of Germany
in 1630, during the Thirty Years War.
By the time of his death in battle in
1632, the king had ensured the survival
of German Protestantism and launched
Sweden as a major European power.

THE NORTHERN SAGA

To the ancient Greeks and Romans, on their warm Mediterranean shores, the Scandinavian world was a cold and mysterious territory, inhabited—in the words of the poet Homer—by "an unhappy race whom endless night invades". The Greek explorer Pythias told tales of a strange, far off northern isle called Thule, where there was no night at the summer solstice and no day in winter. But the remoteness of this hyperborean region, and the rigours of its climate, discouraged potential invaders. Indeed, one of the most striking features of Scandinavia's history is the long continuity of settlement by descendants of its earliest inhabitants. By comparison with the rest of Europe, few alien ethnic groups came in to conquer or displace the original population. As a result, modern Scandinavians have a better idea than people in most other parts of the world as to who their ancestors were, and what they looked like.

Remarkably, a number of these ancestors have been recovered, almost intact, from the peat bogs of Denmark. An Iron Age man found at Tollund, in Jutland, in 1950 is regarded by archaeologists as having the best-preserved human head to have survived from that era anywhere in the world. Though he was buried some 2,000 years ago, preservative acids in the peat have kept his skin unbroken, his hair intact, his features lifelike, his leather cap almost new. The head is now on display in the Silkeborg Museum in central Jutland where, in the words of a leading authority on bog people, modern Scandinavians curious about their forebears can find themselves "face to face with an Iron Age man".

A large number of finds associated with these early people have enabled archaeologists to reconstruct the lifestyle of the early tillers of Scandinavian soil. They lived in village communities or in isolated farmsteads, where they grew barley as a staple crop and raised small herds of sheep and cattle. Their houses had walls of turf, floors of clay and roofs of either straw or thatched heather. They stabled their animals at one end of the longhouses to provide themselves with extra warmth in the bitterly cold winters; in addition, they had open hearths on which they made peat and wood fires whose smoke found its way out through a simple hole in the gable. Along the coasts there were fishermen, using nets as much as 20 metres long to haul up the riches of the sea. Their boats, some of them more than 21 metres in length, were made of oak and had room for 20 to 30 rowers.

The women wore handspun dresses with full skirts and short capes—some of these garments, too, have been found immaculately preserved in the peat bogs. In Copenhagen's National Museum, it is possible to encounter Bronze Age princesses, five or six hundred years older than Tollund Man. Though their features have been somewhat ravaged by time, their gold trinkets still glitter, and their amber beads still glow about them.

It was this precious amber—which is fossilized tree resin, 40 to 60 million years old—that helped bring Scandinavia into contact with the rest of Europe. Centuries before the birth of Christ, pieces of this priceless substance, gathered on the shores of the North Sea and the Baltic, were conveyed slowly to Greece and Rome along a network of overland and river routes. Eventually, Mediterranean mariners ventured northwards through the straits of Gibraltar in search of simpler means of obtaining it. Pliny the Elder mentions a Roman sea captain who visited the Baltic coast in about 60 A.D. to buy amber for the Emperor Nero.

The traders who carried the amber south—along with furs to adorn the rich Romans and slaves to serve them—returned with Mediterranean gold and luxury goods from the Roman Empire's workshops. Roman silver and bronze vessels decorated the homes of local chieftains and were buried with them in their graves; Roman money and jewels made their appearance in the households of wealthy Scandinavian traders and farmers. By the second century, the imperial currency had been carried as far north as present-day Finland, where archaeologists have unearthed coins minted in the reign of the Emperor Hadrian, who ruled Rome from 117 to 134 A.D.

With the decline and ultimate fall of the Empire, in 476 A.D., however, came the epoch of the great migrations that changed the ethnic composition of Europe. Many of the warlike Germanic tribes migrating south and west are thought to have stemmed from Scandinavia—among them the Goths from the Baltic coast, the Teutons (a people work, depicting strange animals, serpents and intricate, abstract designs.

These people must have been engaged in numerous conflicts among themselves. The remains of fortified earthworks dotting the coasts of Denmark and southern Sweden speak of dangerous times, as do the caches of treasure buried nearby. For the most part, they kept to their lands. But late in the eighth century, the Scandinavians burst like a thunderbolt upon an unsuspecting world. From 800 until the middle of the 11th century, these formerly obscure northerners would be the most powerful force in Western Europe. The Age of the Vikings was about to begin.

Early one spring morning, in 793 A.D., a band of heathen seafarers landed at the "holy isle" of Lindisfarne, off the coast of north-east England, and launched an attack upon the island's wealthy monastery. As one chronicler reported, the raiders "came to the church of Lindisfarne, laid everything waste with grievous plundering, trampled the holy places with polluted feet, dug up the altars and seized all the treasures of the holy church. They killed some of the friars, some they took away in fetters, many they drove out, naked and loaded with insults, and some they drowned in the sea."

Such scenes were repeated innumerable times as all of the neighbouring coasts began to feel the keen edge of the Viking sword and battle axe. They sacked villages and monasteries in England, the Hebrides, Ireland and Wales; they robbed and raped along the coasts of Germany, the Low Countries and northern France, even sailing up the Seine and terrorizing the inland settlements, rampaging through Rouen

from the Danish district of Ty) and, from Jutland, the Vandals.

With whole populations on the move, plundering the treasures of the sacked Empire, a substantial amount of the precious metal gradually found its way northwards. In Scandinavia itself, the centuries after the fall of Rome were not merely a turbulent "dark age", but, as one historian describes it, a "veritable age of gold for the northern barbarians". Scandinavian craftsmen of the sixth, seventh and eighth centuries produced striking gold decorations and pendants, some of them imitations of Roman coins. Equally impressive were their bronze ornaments, notably brooches of engraved or filigree

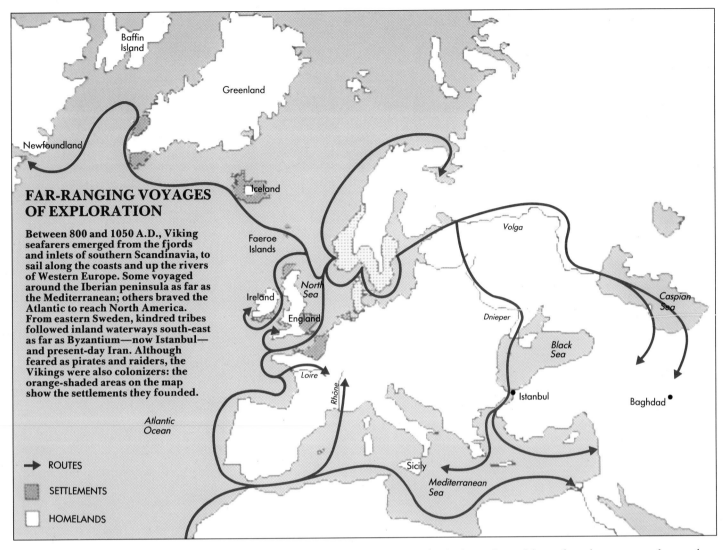

FAR-RANGING VOYAGES OF EXPLORATION

Between 800 and 1050 A.D., Viking seafarers emerged from the fjords and inlets of southern Scandinavia, to sail along the coasts and up the rivers of Western Europe. Some voyaged around the Iberian peninsula as far as the Mediterranean; others braved the Atlantic to reach North America. From eastern Sweden, kindred tribes followed inland waterways south-east as far as Byzantium—now Istanbul— and present-day Iran. Although feared as pirates and raiders, the Vikings were also colonizers: the orange-shaded areas on the map show the settlements they founded.

→ ROUTES

▨ SETTLEMENTS

☐ HOMELANDS

Baffin Island

Greenland

Newfoundland

Iceland

Faeroe Islands

Ireland

North Sea

England

Volga

Dnieper

Caspian Sea

Black Sea

Istanbul

Baghdad

Loire

Rhône

Atlantic Ocean

Sicily

Mediterranean Sea

and putting Paris to the torch. Where there was wealth to take, they took it; where there was only poverty, they took slaves instead. Those who resisted were slaughtered.

The perpetrators of the earliest raids were farmers from Norwegian fjords and the coasts of present-day Denmark. In the summer months, between the spring sowing and the autumn harvest, they ventured out on expeditions in quest of riches and manly honour, leaving the women to run the farms.

These Norsemen called the seasonal forays "going a-viking". The origins of the term are uncertain: it may derive from a word in their Old Norse tongue for deep coastal creeks and inlets.

Vikings loved battle for its own sake and loved sailing the northern seas in their swift longships, with high prows, sleek keels, and flexible, seaworthy hulls. In these splendid craft, 80 or 90 men could slip into an alien harbour by night, to surprise the sleeping inhabitants by the first light of dawn.

What horses were to the Huns, their ships were to the northern marauders. "My mother once told me," says one of their ancient poems, "she'd buy me a longship, a handsome-oared vessel to go sailing with Vikings: to stand at the stern-post and steer a fine warship, then head back for harbour and hew down some foemen."

However, nervous monks and panic-stricken villagers notwithstanding, the Vikings were not just destroyers. In time they became traders, colonizers, and—thanks to their brilliant seamanship—explorers. Short seasonal forays turned into longer expeditions. And for every Norseman who amused himself by wreaking havoc abroad while the crops were growing at home, there was

THE OSEBERG SHIP: TOMB OF A VIKING QUEEN

Covered for a millennium by a mound of stone and turf, the Oseberg ship is one of Scandinavia's greatest archaeological treasures. The ship, excavated at Oseberg farm, near Oslo, in 1904, had been a royal burial place; the grave-goods found within have made it a valuable source of information about the arts, crafts and culture of the early Viking Age.

Historians have suggested that the Oseberg ship may have been the tomb of Queen Asa, who was abducted and forcibly married to Gudrod the Magnificent, a Norwegian ruler. According to legend, she hated Gudrod and had him murdered as he lay in a drunken stupor. She assumed his throne until her death in about 850, when her body was placed in a ship brought ashore from Oslo fjord. Archaeological evidence indicates that the burial dates from this period.

The ship is clearly the burial place of an important personage. Two female skeletons were found, one of them possibly a maidservant who was sacrificed as part of the funeral ritual. The remains were surrounded by personal possessions—looms, beds and kitchen utensils—which might comfort or serve a queen in the afterlife. Should her ghost wish to travel, the burial ship had sailing gear, including a mast and a full set of 30 oars, as well as four sleighs and an ornately decorated cart.

In a 1904 photograph, the newly excavated Oseberg ship emerges from the burial mound that had covered it for 1,000 years.

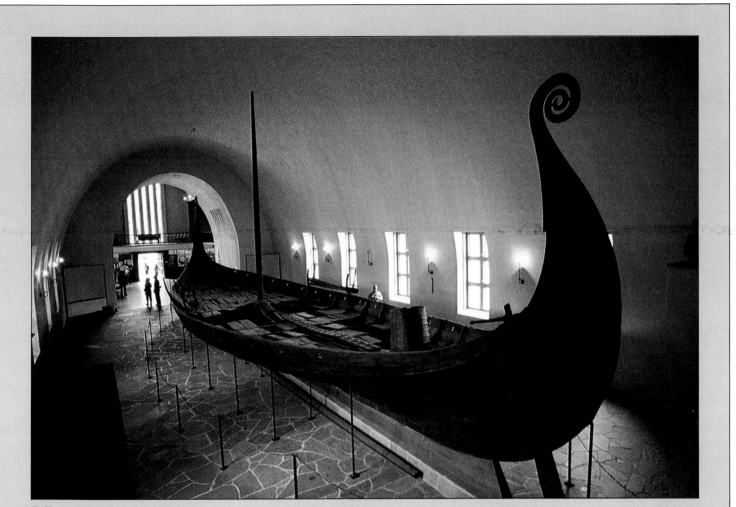

Fully restored, the Oseberg burial ship stands in the Viking Ship Museum in Oslo. Made of oak planking held together with iron rivets, the ship is 21.5 metres long, with an elaborately covered prow and stern soaring 5 metres above the deck.

Decorations on the wooden cart found in the ship suggest that the vehicle, some 5 metres long, was the possession of a wealthy or royal Viking rather than a humble farmer. Carvings on the front depict a man fighting with snakes—possibly a scene from the life of Gunnar, a hero of Norse mythology.

2

another who set off with his entire family or clan on a peaceable migration.

The Scandinavian homelands—at this time only beginning to emerge as three separate nations—were proving inadequate for the support of a growing population. Entire families took to the sea in search of more hospitable territory. The Danes peacefully colonized many coastal areas of eastern England, where hundreds of Danish place names remain today as records of their settlement. The Norsemen were chronically short of arable land; hence they migrated to Orkney, Shetland, the Faeroes, the Hebrides, parts of Ireland, northwest England and Scotland, the Frisian Islands in the North Sea, the Dutch and Belgian river estuaries, and the French coasts near the mouth of the Seine—a region that became known as Normandy after the French kings formally ceded it to a group of Norse settlers in 911.

Other Scandinavian emigrants left their homes as the result of blood feuds and wrangles over property. For those weary of quarrels and vendettas (or those well advised to make themselves scarce), the newly discovered country of Iceland offered a place of refuge. Sometime in the middle of the ninth century, Norse sailors, blown off course by storms, had made landfall on its desolate, forbidding coastline, and eventually found their way home, bringing tales of virgin territory, 900 kilometres west of Norway. When other Vikings began to explore the land with an eye to settlement, however, they may have found a scattering of Irish monks living as hermits.

By 900, an estimated 15,000 to 20,000 people, from mainland Norway and the Norse colonies in Ireland, had settled in Iceland. They were led by 38 chieftains who brought with them their entire households, including families and tenants, retainers and thralls (meaning slaves). In about the year 930, the heads of these first families of Iceland established the Althing, a lawmaking council of elders that evolved into a parliament and has functioned almost without interruption ever since; an institution by the same name still exists as the government of the modern republic of Iceland.

The Icelanders, in their long winter nights, became a nation of storytellers, recording the great events of their day in the prose narratives known as sagas. Originating from the 11th century onwards, and passed down orally by generations of long-memoried bards, these tales paint a richly detailed picture of

Viking life: blood feuds, domestic dramas of the kitchen and the farmyard, foolhardy exploits, and the adventurous voyages of discovery.

The rest of Europe marvelled at the stories it heard about Iceland's natural wonders. "Here there is a strange spring from whose water there rises a fuming stench which changes all it touches to stone though it keeps its first form and shape," reported the 12th-century Danish historian Saxo Grammaticus. "There are also here many wells and streams which from time to time overflow their waters and shoot them high into the air, spraying with white foam all that is near at hand . . . On this same island there is the mountain of Hekla which forever burns and flames. It is a wonder that the mountain, which is covered on all sides with ice and snow, can nevertheless find enough fuel for its continuous and unquenching fire." Perhaps most miraculous of all, "there are also springs in which the water tastes of beer".

One of the settlers on this remarkable island, Erik the Red, was banished from Iceland for three years by a local court, after a blood feud with a neighbour. Spurred on by sailors' tales of an enormous landmass lying far to the west, he and a small band of followers set forth from Iceland in the summer of 982, sailed due west for 320 kilometres and landed in Greenland, populated only by roving Eskimos. During the years of his enforced exile, Erik explored the glaciers, fjords and Arctic meadows of the new-found country. When his term of banishment ended, he returned to Iceland, gathered up a band of potential settlers, and led them back to Greenland in 986. Encouraged by Erik, they established a colony on the coastlands of its south-western tip,

Depicted in a 1510 hymnal, St. Birgitta of Sweden receives the rules of a new monastic order from Jesus and Mary. Birgitta, a visionary who died in 1373, was concerned with world events as well as theology, advising the Pope on European politics and proposing a plan to end the Hundred Years War.

2

along fjords teeming with fish.

In the year 1000, Erik's son Leif Eriksson, alias Leif the Lucky, sailed even further west, and discovered a land he called Vinland—according to his saga—"because vines producing excellent wine grow wild there; moreover, self-sown wheat grows there in abundance". He and his crew had discovered America, five centuries before Columbus. Although the place where they landed has yet to be identified, archaeologists have unearthed Viking remains further north, well beyond the grape-growing area, at the northernmost tip of Newfoundland.

The Vikings were too few in number, however, to maintain themselves in North America. Even the Greenland colony, which grew to an estimated 3,000 to 5,000 settlers, eventually lost contact with Europe. When Norwegian explorers returned, late in the 17th century, there was no longer any sign of people other than the native Eskimos. The settlers' fate remains a mystery: they may have been defeated by a rapidly deteriorating climate, been absorbed by the Eskimo population or, as an Eskimo oral tradition suggests, there may have been quarrels during which the Norsemen were wiped out.

Throughout the Viking Age, while the Norwegians and Danes had looked westwards to the Atlantic, Swedish adventurers—known as the Varangians—turned their attentions eastwards, to the lands across the Baltic Sea. They travelled south from Lake Ladoga and over the watershed to the Volga, the Don and the Dnieper in order to trade iron, furs and slaves for Saracen silver and gold. Some stopped to establish local kingdoms, first at Novgorod, within easy reach of the Baltic Sea, then at Kiev, two thirds of the

way to the Black Sea. The indigenous population called the interlopers Rus, possibly from an early word for "horse"—which eventually led to the whole nation being called Russia.

During the summer of 921, an emissary of the Caliph at Baghdad, one Ibn Fadlan, encountered a group of Vikings who were encamped along the shores of the Volga. He stayed with them long enough to write a lengthy, detailed description of them as a sort of intelligence report for his government. Since Ibn Fadlan was an educated man, schooled in the courtly customs of one of the world's most fastidious civilizations, he was rather taken aback by the bed and table-manners of these incredibly bumptious barbarians. What makes his report all the more fascinating is that it constitutes the only extant account of life among the Vikings when they were not raiding and plundering, as well as the only description of the Vikings as seen through the eyes of a more or less neutral observer.

"I saw the Rus who were there for commerce and come down the river Atul (Volga)," he writes. "I have never seen bodies more perfect than theirs. One would say they are as tall as palm

trees . . . Everyone carries an axe, sword and knife . . . They are the filthiest people under God. They never wash off excrement or urine; they do not wash after sexual relations, they do not wash their hands after meals. They are like wild donkeys . . . With them are beautiful young female slaves intended for the slave merchants."

Elsewhere in Europe, however, there were powerful civilizing forces at work among the Scandinavian immigrants. The early Vikings had been pagans, untouched by the missionary monks who had brought the Christian faith to the rest of Western Europe several centuries before. But, as early as the ninth century, some of the Norsemen who settled among the Franks were converted to Christianity. The Danish chieftains who established the occupied territory known as the Danelaw in north and east England were soon baptized and buried in Christian churches. Olaf Cuaran, the ruler of Dublin from 941 to 980, also became a Christian. Finally, towards the end of the 10th century, the kings of Denmark, Norway and Sweden were converted to the new faith, after years of patient efforts by missionary monks. Their sub-

jects rapidly followed the kings into the
Christian faith, sometimes persuaded
by sermons, sometimes by swords. The
Icelandic Althing agreed to accept
Christianity about the year 1000—
though with due allowance for the con-
tinuation of some of the traditional
pagan practices.

It was not a difficult shift for most
people: in place of the cruciform amulet
known as "Thor's hammer", which
they had always worn around their
necks, they now wore the symbol of
Christ's cross. Their names for most of
the days of the week remained the
same, still consecrated to the pagan
gods: Tiu's day, of the god of war and
the sky; Wodin's day, of the one-eyed
chief of the gods; Thor's day, dedicated
to the god of Thunder, and Frigg's day,
which belonged to Wodin's wife, the
goddess of the heavens.

By the 11th century, Scandinavia
was dotted with Christian churches,
many of them built on the sites of the
old pagan burial mounds and holy
places. Though the new creed did not
prevent them from making war on their
neighbours, the Scandinavian kings
were now Christian monarchs and
therefore subject to the moral restraints
of the medieval church. Monastic foundations multiplied; travelling architects from Germany, France, Italy and
England came to construct stone
churches; nunneries and hospitals were
founded; and the Scandinavian faithful
pilgrimaged along routes still trodden
today to their first shrine—that of St.
Olaf in Trondheim.

Increasingly, Christian monarchs
such as Harald Bluetooth of Denmark
and Canute (Knut) the Great treated
the church as the one institution that
could bring unity, discipline and prosperity to their strife-torn dominions.

Its teachings reinforced their authority: in the orderly Christian hierarchy,
the king rules over his subjects, but God
rules over the king.

It was Canute who gave his courtiers
the famous object lesson of placing his
throne at the water's edge at low tide
and bidding the sea "not to rise over
my land, and not to presume to wet the
clothes and limbs of your lord". Then,
after the disobedient waves had wetted
his feet, the king jumped back on to dry
land and told his retainers: "Be it
known to all inhabitants of the world
that the power of kings is empty and
superficial, and that no one is worthy of
the name of king except for Him whose
will is obeyed by Heaven, earth and sea
in accordance with eternal laws."

In the year 1066, King Harald Har-

drada of Norway made one last attempt
to invade England in order to wrest the
crown from its newly proclaimed king,
Harold Godwinsson, who was himself
the grandson of a Viking raider. Harald
Hardrada was killed in action near
York and his army thrown back into
the sea. But only three weeks later, at
Hastings, Harold Godwinsson himself
was killed and his army routed by
10,000 men led by Duke William of
Normandy, another invader who had
Viking blood in his veins.

William subsequently took systema-
tic measures to protect his new realm
against attacks from Norway or Denmark, securing the coast with a chain of
well-armed fortresses. Never again was
England threatened by a large-scale
Scandinavian invasion.

The following centuries of Scandinavian history were marked by political
concerns much closer to home. The an-
nals of the later Middle Ages speak of
shifting rivalries and alliances in a
three-sided struggle for power among
the kings of Denmark, Norway and
Sweden, and of frequent warfare
against hostile neighbours.

At the same time, the Scandinavian
climate was becoming markedly colder; by the late 1300s, northern Europe
was entering a "Little Ice Age" that
was to last for the next 400 years. With
deteriorating climatic conditions, the
food crops repeatedly failing, animals
suffering correspondingly, the population throughout the Scandinavian
world declined. Iceland, according to
the tax records of 1096, had only 50,000
inhabitants, and the island's population probably remained at that level for
several centuries.

Many previously cultivated areas
were abandoned, and the overall area
of settlement contracted as famine and

The sandy beard and aggressive
stance of Gustavus I Vasa are
captured by the contemporary artist,
Willem Boy. After leading a revolt
against the Danes, Vasa was elected
king by the Swedish nobility in 1523.

A CHRONOLOGY OF KEY EVENTS

c. 8,000 B.C. As the Ice Ages wane, the earliest migrants enter Scandinavia, living first by hunting and fishing, then by limited agriculture and herding. Settlement is sparse, lagging far behind more southerly regions.

c. 2,000 B.C. New peoples—probably the direct ancestors of today's inhabitants—move northwards into Scandinavia, introducing the use of the axe. Settlement spreads into the forests. Trade develops with the rest of Europe.

1,500–500 B.C. A thriving Bronze Age civilization develops, linked by trade with Mediterranean cultures. Archaeological finds from this period include woollen textiles, gold, jewellery, amber, and the bronze horns known as *lurs*.

450–500 A.D. During the break-up of the western Roman empire, Scandinavia remains outside the main disturbances, but is enriched by plunder that is circulating in barbarian possession. Local warfare occupies the small kingships and loose tribal groupings of the nascent Scandinavian nations.

800–1050 Impelled by over-population at home, Viking crews embark on raiding and trading expeditions affecting most of the Western world. Vikings from Sweden reach Byzantium through Russia; western Vikings from Denmark and Norway plunder and settle European seacoasts and Iceland.

874 Norsemen colonize Iceland.

c.930 Icelandic settlers form a commonwealth, initiating 300 years of self-government.

986 Settlers from Iceland colonize Greenland.

c. 1000 Leif Eriksson leaves Iceland and reaches North America. Christianity is adopted by the Icelandic commonwealth, and by the kings of Norway, Denmark and Sweden.

1017 Canute, later king of Denmark, defeats an English army and becomes king of England.

1120–1230 The Sagas—prose tales of Norse history and legend—are composed in Iceland.

1262 Weakened by economic hardship and internal feuding, Iceland and Greenland come under the rule of the king of Norway.

1293 Finland is conquered and annexed by Sweden.

c. 1350 The Black Death reaches Scandinavia, reducing the population by as much as two thirds in some areas.

1397 Denmark, Norway (with Iceland) and Sweden (with Finland) come under one rule when Queen Margrethe of Denmark creates the Union of Kalmar, and crowns her great-nephew, Eric of Pomerania, king of the three realms.

1477 The first Scandinavian university is founded at Uppsala in Sweden, followed two years later by the University of Copenhagen in Denmark.

1520 In an attempt to quell Swedish resistance to Danish control, King Christian II of Denmark has opponents to his rule murdered in Stockholm.

1523 In reaction to King Christian's tyranny, Sweden revolts from union with Denmark–Norway.

1527 Gustavus I Vasa establishes the Lutheran church in Sweden and Finland. Ten years later, Denmark, together with Norway and Iceland, adopts Lutheranism.

1539 The Swedish priest Olaus Magnus publishes a pictorial map of Scandinavia, followed by a history of the Scandinavian peoples in 1555, giving the rest of Europe its first visual and textual documentation on the lands and peoples of the North.

1563–1570 Denmark–Norway defeats Sweden in the Scandinavian Seven Years War.

1573 The Danish astronomer Tycho Brahe publishes his great work, *De Nova Stella*. With the patronage of King Frederick II, Brahe sets up an observatory where he works for 20 years improving the accuracy of astronomical observations.

1602 Denmark declares trade monopoly over Iceland.

1611–1613 The Kalmar War, a further conflict between Denmark–Norway and Sweden, ends with a treaty marking the start of a period of economic and territorial expansion for Sweden. The nation advances to create a Baltic empire at the expense of Poland and Russia.

1611–1632 Reign of Gustavus II Adolphus. Sweden plays a major part in the Thirty Years War.

1638 Sweden plants a colony in America: Fort Christina on the Delaware River.

1640 A university is founded at Åbo in Finland.

1654 Queen Christina of Sweden abdicates after a 22-year reign, to become a Roman Catholic. Her cousin Charles X becomes king.

1697–1721 Charles XII of Sweden undertakes over-ambitious campaigns against Denmark, Poland, Saxony and Russia, and is killed in battle in 1718. Sweden subsequently loses its powerful position and much of its trans-Baltic territory.

1735 The Swedish naturalist Linnaeus publishes his *Systema Naturae*, the foundation for naming and classifying plant and animal species.

1807 British forces bombard Copenhagen, driving Denmark into alliance with Napoleonic France.

1809 Sweden is forced to cede Finland to Russia; the country becomes a Russian Grand Duchy with limited self-government.

1810 The Swedish parliament elects one of Napoleon's field-marshals—Bernadotte—as heir to the childless Charles XIII. The new crown prince takes the title Karl Johan.

1814 In spite of Norwegian reluctance, Karl Johan secures Norway's separation from Denmark. Although ruled by the king of Sweden, Norway remains a separate state, and retains its own constitution.

1825 The first Norwegian emigrant ship sails to America.

1835–1850 A growing interest in indigenous Scandinavian culture is marked by the publication of Elias

Lönnrot's *Kalevala*—an epic compilation of Finnish folk poems—and the Norwegian folk tales collected by P. C. Asbjørnsen and Jørgen Moe. The folk form is elaborated by the Dane Hans Christian Andersen in his fictional fairy tales.

1844 The first of Denmark's folk high schools brings political and cultural education to rural children.

1864 Denmark, defeated in war by Prussia and Austria, loses the duchies of Schleswig and Holstein—about one third of her territory.

1860–1890 Rural poverty, worsened by crop failures and rising population, drives Swedes, Norwegians, Danes and Finns to emigrate in their thousands to the United States.

1860–1900 A cultural flowering or "northern Renaissance" brings to prominence the writers Ibsen and Strindberg, the painter Munch and the composers Grieg and Sibelius.

1879–1880 The Finnish explorer A. E. Nordenskiöld takes the first ship through the Arctic via the Northeast Passage across the top of Asia.

1888 The Norwegian explorer Fridtjof Nansen makes the first crossing of Greenland, and goes on to complete further polar expeditions.

1905 The union of Norway and Sweden is dissolved. Prince Carl of Denmark is elected ruler of an independent Norway, with the title of King Haakon VII.

1906 After a period of repression and resistance, Russia permits the establishment of a Finnish parliament. Universal suffrage makes Finland the first European nation to give women the vote. Norway soon follows.

1911–1912 Roald Amundsen, a Norwegian, leads the first successful expedition to the South Pole.

1914–1918 The three Scandinavian kingdoms remain neutral during World War I.

1918 Civil war follows Finland's declaration of independence from Russia in December 1917. After leading a volunteer army to victory, General Carl Gustaf Mannerheim becomes regent of an independent Finland.

1918 Iceland becomes independent under a Danish–Icelandic monarchy.

1925 The Swedish star Greta Garbo makes her film debut.

1933–1936 Sweden sets up state social welfare schemes. Denmark institutes major public works programmes for relief of unemployment. Norway introduces state old-age pensions and unemployment insurance.

1939–1940 At the outset of World War II, Denmark and Norway are occupied by Germany. Iceland is occupied by the Western allies. Finland goes to war with the Soviet Union, while Sweden stays neutral.

1944 Iceland declares independence from Denmark.

1948 After Finland undertakes to pay war reparations to the Soviet Union, the two nations sign a Treaty of Friendship, Co-operation and Mutual Assistance.

1949 Norway, Denmark and Iceland join NATO.

1952 Denmark, Norway, Iceland and Sweden form the Nordic Council for economic, social and cultural co-operation. Finland joins the Council three years later.

1958 Iceland and Britain clash over fishing rights in the first "cod war". Hostilities end in 1976 when Britain accepts Iceland's 322-kilometre fishing limit.

1980 Iceland elects the world's first woman president, Vigdis Finnbogadottir. In Sweden, a deadlock in private and public sector wage negotiations creates the worst labour dispute in the nation's history, with 25 per cent of the work force on strike or locked out.

1981 Norway puts into production her recently discovered reserves of North Sea oil and gas, which give her some protection from the worldwide economic depression hampering the other Nordic countries.

pestilence stalked the land, inspiring the "Dance of Death" paintings that still decorate medieval Scandinavian church walls. In these grotesque reminders of mortality a grinning Grim Reaper leads his victims in a dance—young and old, rich and poor, king, priest and peasant alike, all forced to tread his measure. This was the time of the Black Death—bubonic plague, carried by ship around the coasts of Europe—which devastated much of Scandinavia; in some parts of Norway, two thirds of the populace was wiped out in a matter of months.

It was during this tumultuous era that Finland was drawn into the Scandinavian sphere. Living in small communities along the coasts, around the island-dotted lakes or along the banks of fast-flowing rivers, the Finns were peasant farmers, hunters, fishers and modest fur traders. Ruled by no king and defended by no army, they were fair game for invaders.

Between the 11th and the 14th centuries, Swedish armies marched into Finland for purposes that were missionary as well as military. With the blessing of the Pope in Rome, Swedish crusaders converted Finland's pagan population to Christianity, and began a process of political and cultural domination that lasted until the 19th century.

These crusades were motivated, at least in part, by the need to fend off dangerous influences from the East: missionaries from Russia who were entering Finland and spreading the Eastern Orthodox version of the Christian faith, a spiritual as well as a secular threat to the power of the Roman Catholic church. As they advanced, the Swedish invaders consolidated their position by constructing a chain of fortresses at strategic points along the southern coasts of Finland.

Under the influence of their Swedish conquerors, the Finns were drawn into the orbit of the emerging culture of the Renaissance. Before the first Scandinavian universities were founded—at Uppsala in 1477 and Copenhagen in 1479—Finnish and Swedish students regularly made their way to Paris, where some of them obtained masters' degrees, or attended German universities, returning to their own lands with the fruits of the new humanist movements in science and arts.

But German influence, in particular, extended far beyond cultural exchange. During the 14th century, most of Scandinavia's growing maritime trade was controlled by the powerful association of German merchants known as the Hanseatic League, which managed to impose its will on the kings of Denmark, Norway and Sweden by force of arms. The League comprised a multinational chain of 70 member cities stretching from Nantes to Novgorod. It dominated Baltic commerce from Lübeck, the richest of all the Hanseatic towns, and established German trading enclaves in the principal Scandinavian commercial centres, such as Bergen's Tyskebryggen—the "German Quay"—lined with the well-filled warehouses of the League. In some of the Gothic churches built by the Hanseatic merchants, services were to be conducted in German for several hundred years.

The concluding years of the 14th century brought with them a turning point in Nordic history—the Union of Three Crowns, sometimes called the Union of Kalmar, under Queen Margrethe in 1397. Margrethe, a daughter of the King of Denmark, married the King of Norway, and became regent of

A 17th-century painting shows a red carpet stretching from Copenhagen Castle to the dais where Frederick III, illumined by a shaft of sunlight, is being declared Denmark's first absolute and hereditary king. On the far left is the artist, the deaf-mute Wolfgang Heimbach, waving his hat.

both countries following the death of her husband and her son, the infant Danish king. By dint of shrewd diplomacy—and a disputed family claim to the Swedish crown—she soon persuaded the Swedes, too, to accept her as "Sovereign Lady and Ruler". To weld the three kingdoms together, Margrethe arranged for her infant kinsman, Eric of Pomerania, to be crowned king of Denmark, Norway and Sweden. Under his rule the three states retained their own laws and customs, and were administered by their own dignitaries: it was a union of crowns rather than kingdoms, that was to last—despite internal dissensions and a period of secession by the disgruntled Swedes—for over 100 years.

The Union of Three Crowns was finally brought to an end in the early 1500s through the misuse of royal authority by King Christian II. Determined to break the power of the nobles, Christian attempted to play off the merchant class against the landed aristocracy. But in Sweden, he met with resistance from all sectors of the population, and the Swedish delegates to the assembly of notables that gathered in Copenhagen in 1513 flatly refused to recognize Christian as their king. "We have," they declared, "the choice between peace at home and strife here, or peace here and civil war at home, and we prefer the former."

Christian promptly launched a series of campaigns to bring Sweden to heel, but not until 1520 did he succeed in occupying Stockholm and compelling the local nobles to recognize his sovereignty. Then, after three days of banqueting, he gave a pre-arranged signal to a troop of Danish soldiers, and they

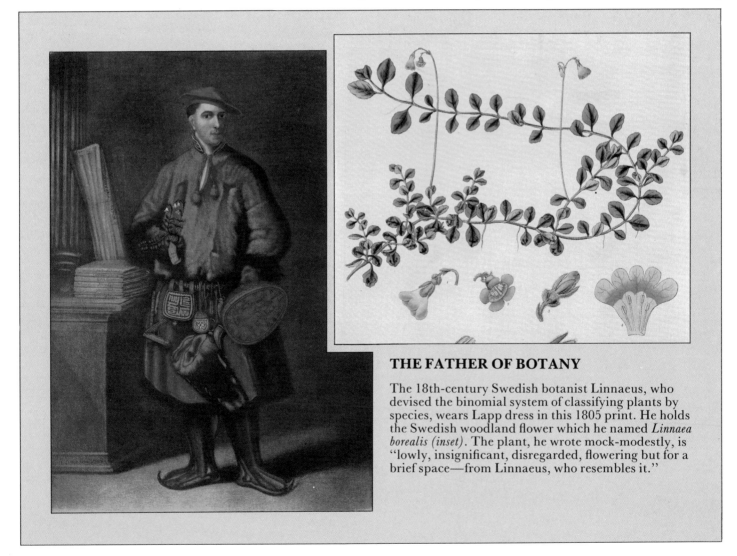

THE FATHER OF BOTANY

The 18th-century Swedish botanist Linnaeus, who devised the binomial system of classifying plants by species, wears Lapp dress in this 1805 print. He holds the Swedish woodland flower which he named *Linnaea borealis (inset)*. The plant, he wrote mock-modestly, is "lowly, insignificant, disregarded, flowering but for a brief space—from Linnaeus, who resembles it."

arrested the invited guests—his former adversaries. Scores of Swedish leaders, including nobles, bishops, burgomasters and town councillors, were later beheaded or drowned in what came to be known as "the Stockholm Bloodbath". In all, about 600 people were slaughtered, and the corpses of opponents already buried were exhumed so that they could be burnt on a pyre with the rest. Later, Christian explained his policies by saying, "Mild measures are of no use; the remedies that give the whole body a good shaking are the best and surest."

The king's tyrannies produced the inevitable backlash: Sweden rose in revolt, and when Christian attempted to coerce Denmark and Norway into a war against the breakaway kingdom, they too renounced their allegiance and offered the Danish–Norwegian crown to Christian's uncle, Duke Frederick of Holstein. Eventually Christian was forced to surrender to his rival, and for the last 27 years of his life was kept in solitary confinement.

After the collapse of the union, Denmark and Norway remained together as a single realm, a relationship that would last until 1814.

In Sweden, the aftermath of the Stockholm massacre and Christian's downfall was the election of a new king, Gustavus I Vasa, by an assembly representing the nobles, clergy and commoners of the realm. Gustavus' reign opened an irreparable breach with the Vatican: his own father had been murdered on the orders of the bishop of Stockholm, formerly adviser to the deposed tyrant Christian, and an implacable enmity grew up between the Papacy and the new regime.

Although Gustavus I held no strong theological opinions, the rift caused

him to side with Germany's Lutherans. Within a decade the newly independent Swedish nation had become one of the great strongholds of Protestantism, and Finland—as the eastern wing of Sweden—followed suit.

In the 16th century, Sweden and Denmark–Norway established themselves as formidable naval powers. Denmark controlled the entrance to the Baltic, collecting tolls at the strategically sited Kronborg Castle, at Helsingør—the Elsinore of Shakespeare's *Hamlet*—where the Sound is at its narrowest part. Standing guard over these straits, the Danes levied tribute on foreign shipping until 1857.

Sweden, on the other hand, enjoyed a monopoly of such naval stores as

pitch and "Stockholm tar"; in an age of wooden ships, no European merchant fleets or navies could survive without these essential materials for waterproofing their vessels. Sweden was also Europe's main source of the pig iron and copper ingots used for the manufacture of bronze cannon and other military hardware.

As the two rival states grew in strength, their contest for the domination of the Baltic intensified. In a bid to acquire new domains on the eastern shore of the sea, Sweden became embroiled in the affairs of Poland and Russia, fighting now on one side, now on the other, in accordance with shifts in the balance of power. But, for the time being, Denmark was mistress of

2

the seas. So powerful was her fleet during the latter half of the 16th century that Frederick II was able to enforce a rule that all foreign ships should strike their topsails when meeting a Danish man-of-war.

Twice the competing nations measured their strength on the battlefield. In the Scandinavian Seven Years War from 1563 to 1570, and in the Kalmar War from 1611 to 1613 (so-called after the hotly contended fortress of that name), Denmark–Norway emerged the victor on both occasions. But the second of these conflicts ended with a treaty that brought peace for a time to the competing nations. Each rival returned the territories it had conquered, though Sweden was compelled to pay the Danes a massive indemnity.

The young Swedish king, Gustavus II Adolphus, whose reign began at the start of the Kalmar War, was to play a key role in the subsequent era of expansion. During his 21-year reign, from 1611 to 1632, Sweden was to become virtually an empire, as displayed in the magnificent baroque maps of his realm which were drawn for him at this time. The kingdom now entered into a golden age of increased prosperity at home and prestige abroad that would last for the rest of the 17th century.

Sweden's growing might derived not only from the kingdom's natural resources but also from the fact that it was one of the most efficient European states of the day. Important factors in its political success were its military and naval efficiency, its governmental organization and its adoption of the latest technological innovations.

Accordingly, Gustavus II Adolphus was destined to become one of the few successful Protestant generals of the Thirty Years War that devastated cen-

tral Europe between 1618 and 1648. In 1630, he led an army of 16,000 Swedes into Germany to deliver the Lutherans from tyranny. Within months he had defeated the far more powerful forces of the Habsburg Emperor Ferdinand II, and had made himself master of Germany from Saxony to the Rhine. After two years of campaigning, however, Gustavus was killed on the battlefield of Lützen, just as he was about to win another hard-fought victory. His heart was sent home to Sweden, wrapped in a silken shirt.

Gustavus II Adolphus was 37 at his death: his only child, daughter of a Prussian princess, was the six-year-old Princess Christina, who grew up to be a brilliantly gifted but also headstrong and extravagant queen. "Her majesty is not like women-folk," declared her chief minister, Axel Oxenstierna, when she was only 15, "but is stout-hearted and of good understanding so that, if she be not corrupted, we have good hopes for her."

When she succeeded to the throne in her 18th year (the silver throne made for her coronation is still used by the king of Sweden when he opens the Swedish parliament), Christina did her best to bring the Thirty Years War to an end—if only because peace would allow her to jettison the officious and overbearing Oxenstierna. At home she ruled with a lavish but energetic hand, encouraging trade and manufacturing, and ennobling members of the middle class. Abroad, her sea captains attempted to plant the seeds of an American empire: Swedish and Dutch settlers established Fort Christina at the mouth of the Delaware River, where Wilmington is today.

But in her late twenties, Christina grew weary of affairs of state and re-

belled at the idea of submitting to the will of her cousin, who was waiting in the wings to become her husband. Instead of marrying him she designated him her successor—Charles X—and, in 1654, performed the solemn act of abdication, in which she placed her own crown on Charles's head.

Still fêted as a queen, Christina journeyed to Rome, converted to Catholicism with pomp and circumstance, and then proceeded to scandalize the Pope and Roman aristocracy with her hedonistic lifestyle. She lived lavishly in the Farnese palace on a Swedish state pension, collecting art and exploring antiquities by day, and giving notoriously debauched parties by night.

By the middle of the 17th century, Sweden had emerged as a major military power. It was now one of the largest states of Europe, with about twice as much territory as it has today. Much of it had been acquired from Denmark–Norway, whose power was fast receding: not until the 18th century did the pendulum swing back again, so that a certain equilibrium was re-established between the Danes and the Swedes.

Ironically, it was one of the boldest, most ambitious of Sweden's rulers who presided over the empire's downfall. Charles XII, in his military adventures against Denmark, Poland, Saxony and Russia, fatally over-extended the human and financial resources of his kingdom. After his death in battle in 1718, his demoralized armies returned home and Sweden was forced to surrender to Russia much of the Baltic territory it had acquired in the years of imperial expansion.

As the empire fell, the threat from the East grew greater. The Swedish Grand Duchy of Finland was devastated by what came to be called "the Great Wrath"—a seven-year period of occupation by Russian troops that ended in 1721. The Northern War which preceded it had already cost Finland most of her young men, and the harshness of the occupation, coupled with widespread crop failure, drove a quarter of the country people from their farms and reduced the population from about 400,000 to under 300,000. One document of the era reads that, in marking the passing of those who died of hunger, "church bells tolled until they cracked". Henceforth Swedish power in Finland was to be increasingly threatened by the growing military and economic might of the Russian tsars.

The pressure on her eastern flank led to one of Sweden's most significant administrative achievements: the compilation of the first modern census. In 1750, partly motivated by a need to anticipate manpower and food resources in case of war, data was collected from every parish, monitoring births, marriages, deaths, causes of mortality and the movements of the population.

Even without the exigencies of national security, the gathering of information was a major passion of the age. In this century of intellectual enlightenment, Swedish science was spurred on by such figures as Linnaeus, the brilliant naturalist, who systematized the study of botany, and Anders Celsius, the astronomer, who invented the centigrade thermometer.

At the same time, the Swedish landed aristocracy acquired new polish and sophistication as patrons of art and letters. Under their sponsorship, Swedish literature and scholarship flourished.

Commissioned by wealthy nobles, local and foreign architects produced a succession of baroque and rococo masterpieces. One of the nation's finest palaces was built during this era, Drottningholm, on the shore of Lake Mälar near Stockholm. This architectural gem incorporating formal gardens, a court theatre and a Chinese summerhouse, was Scandinavia's answer to Versailles, a gathering place for the most glittering artistic, intellectual and musical talents of the day.

The moving spirit behind this lively court was King Gustav III (1746–1792), who founded the Swedish Academy, built the first theatre and opera

2

house in Stockholm, and was himself a famous playwright. The king's career was cut short, however, when he was assassinated at a masked ball held in March 1792, at his own opera house. The murder was the work of a group of disaffected noblemen vainly hoping to regain their eroded powers. Gustav had been warned of the plot beforehand, but stubbornly refused to cancel his engagement. (Half a century later, Giuseppe Verdi composed his opera *Un Ballo in Maschera* to a libretto linked with this incident.)

The assassination of Gustav anticipated the end of an era—the demise of absolutist monarchy in Scandinavia. For over a century both Denmark–Norway and Sweden had been ruled by autocratic sovereigns who professed to derive their authority from "the divine right of kings". Even the isolated, self-reliant Icelanders, whose trade had been subjected to total monopoly by the Danes, suffered from the increasing whims and decrees of the kings of Denmark. However, not all Danish monarchs abused their power. Christian VI, who ruled from 1730 to 1746, was praised by his contemporary, the great Danish playwright Ludwig Holberg, for "a reign of bliss when everything seemed to gain new life and energies".

But by the end of the 18th century, absolutism had clearly run its course. The French Revolution demonstrated to the rest of Europe how easy it was to depose and decapitate a king. But France rapidly found itself in the grip of a no less inexorable absolutist, Napoleon Bonaparte, who was soon at war with most of Europe in his campaign to maintain his power.

Both Sweden and Denmark–Norway were drawn into the maelstrom of the Napoleonic wars, though on opposite sides. Denmark–Norway endeavoured to remain neutral in the bitter conflict between Britain and France, but the British navy twice intervened in order to prevent the Danish fleet from falling into French hands, and to maintain open access to the supply of essential naval stores. In 1807, a British expeditionary force under the command of Lord Nelson landed in Denmark and seized the Danish fleet almost intact. In retaliation, Denmark made common cause with Napoleon and remained his faithful ally until his defeat at the battle of Leipzig in 1813.

Sweden, meanwhile, found itself at war against Russia, France and Denmark–Norway. In 1808, Russian troops invaded Finland and occupied the whole of the Grand Duchy. In the wake of this defeat the young, inept Swedish King Gustav IV was deposed and replaced by his elderly uncle Charles XIII. It was Charles who acceded to the 1809 Treaty of Frederikshamn, which yielded the Grand Duchy of Finland to Russia—henceforth Alexander I of Russia would wear a second crown, as Grand Duke of Finland.

Since Charles was only a stopgap king, childless and infirm, the Swedish parliament made repeated attempts to find a candidate for the succession. The choice fell on one of Napoleon's most capable—and disaffected—field marshals, Jean-Baptiste Bernadotte, who was popular in Stockholm due to the kindness he had shown towards the Swedish prisoners in the war with Denmark. Soon after his arrival in the Swedish capital in 1810, he was elected Crown Prince and formally adopted as a son by the elderly, failing king. He chose to be called Karl Johan.

During the final years of the Napoleonic wars, Karl Johan—whose relations with Napoleon had always been stormy—turned against his former chief to command the Swedish army in the field. In 1813 he headed the northern front in the critical campaign that led to Bonaparte's defeat at Leipzig. Within a year he had also achieved his principal ambition—that of severing Norway from Denmark and attaching it to Sweden.

Denmark—defeated in war and officially bankrupt—had no choice but to consent to the new arrangement. To some extent the Danes were compensated for their loss by receiving Swedish Pomerania (on the southern coast of the Baltic Sea); they were also permitted to retain the old Norse colonies of Iceland, Greenland and the Faeroe Islands. The Norwegians, however, had not been consulted, and acknowledged their new rulers only after Karl Johan invaded their country with Swedish troops in 1814. In the ensuing compromise, Norway was proclaimed "a free, independent and indivisible kingdom united with Sweden under one king". It was accorded its own constitution, and the right to elect its own parliament, the Storting, with freedom to legislate internal affairs with little interference from the Swedish crown.

Partly in response to these political developments, the people of Norway and Finland began to assert their national identities. Inspired by the romantic nationalism, the Norwegians and Finns set about rediscovering their literary past and codifying their written languages. In Norway, the folklorists Asbjørnsen and Moe began to collect the old rural tales and legends; and the romantic scenic canvases of artist J.C. Dahl captured the rugged grandeur of the Norwegian landscape. Meanwhile, the official Danish language of administration and the courts, *Riksmål*, now called *Bokmål*, was complemented by the vernacular of the Norwegian country people—*Landsmål* or *Nynorsk*, as it came to be called.

In Finland, long under foreign linguistic as well as political domination, the national revival of the native language—and the creation of literary Finnish—was given impetus in 1835 by the first publication of *Kalevala*. This collection of ancient folk poetry had been passed on orally through generations of storytellers and put together by the apothecary Elias Lönnrot. Fin-

nish, which had been recognized as an official language jointly with Swedish and Russian in 1860, eventually became a central feature in the struggle against Russian rule. But while the Finnish language fostered a new sense of nationhood, it also opened a serious split between the Finnish-speaking majority and the Swedish-speaking minority within the Grand Duchy.

Elsewhere in Europe, the 19th century ushered in an epoch of big-power politics, and the Scandinavian nations were forced to adjust to a considerably diminished role: after some 300 years

as military and diplomatic powers to be reckoned with, Sweden and Denmark now found themselves buffeted by international events they could no longer influence or control. Denmark, for example, lost about a third of its territory when Prussia's "Iron Chancellor", Otto von Bismarck, initiated a brief war between Prussia and Denmark in 1864. Hostilities ended with Germany annexing Slesvig (Schleswig) and Holstein, two duchies that had formed part of the Danish monarchy for 500 years.

But what 19th-century Denmark lost in temporal power, it more than made up in intellectual prestige—thanks to scientists such as H. C. Ørsted, writers such as Søren Kierkegaard and Hans Christian Andersen, and artists such as the sculptor Bertel Thorvaldsen. This "northern Renaissance" also extended to the rest of Scandinavia: the Norwegian playwright Henrik Ibsen and the Swedish author August Strindberg revolutionized European ideas of theatre just as the Norwegian painter Edvard Munch helped launch the Expressionist movement in art, and composers such as Jan Sibelius in Finland and Carl Nielsen in Denmark extended the range of symphonic music.

In spite of this creative ferment, many of the Scandinavians still regarded themselves as backwoodsmen—for example, the Danish writer Georg Brandes (1842–1927) reflected that "in the North, one had the feeling of being shut off from the intellectual life of the time". Indeed, many of the region's great artists chose to spend the major part of their careers abroad, searching for a livelihood.

But the latter part of the 19th century saw a much larger exodus of people: the massive emigration to the U.S. and Canada, popularly—if somewhat

In a tempera painting by the Finnish artist Gallén-Kallela, the jealous Joukahainen waits, bow in hand, to ambush Väinämöinen, the hero of Finland's national epic, the *Kalevala*. This compilation of ballads, published in 1835, inspired a new awareness of Finnish language and culture.

2

Haakon VII, first king of an independent Norway for 500 years, poses with Queen Maud and Prince Olav for a portrait in 1909. A Danish prince, Haakon was offered the throne by the Norwegian parliament after the union with Sweden ended in 1905.

melodramatically—known as the "Great Bloodletting". As the populations of Sweden, Denmark, Norway and Finland virtually doubled between 1800 and 1900, so did the pressure on available resources. For peasants from the rocky and unyielding soils of Småland in southern Sweden and Danes from the barren heathland of Jutland, leaving their homelands seemed to be the only solution.

In 1870, one in 10 of all immigrants to the United States came from the Scandinavian countries, and the flood did not subside until the beginning of World War I. Among them were many Finnish and Norwegian farmers, who were driven from their homes by the periodic famines that still ravaged northern agriculture.

In the lands they had left behind, the seeds of social change were being planted. Thanks to agricultural improvements, such as the increasing use of potatoes and other new root crops, people were better nourished than ever before. They were also healthier: the Jenner method of smallpox vaccination, introduced to Scandinavia at the beginning of the 19th century, was gradually liberating northerners from the ravages of their most dreaded killer-disease. Its effect on small, ill-fed communities had always been devastating; in an 18th-century epidemic, for instance, Iceland had lost an estimated one third of its total population.

With the coming of railways to Denmark in the 1840s, and the development of fast, efficient steamships plying the fjords of Norway, forging more reliable links with Iceland and wending their way between the islands off the Danish and Swedish coasts, communications improved beyond measure. New technologies and products were

carried to the rural hinterlands by the same ships and trains that took people away from the countryside to the more promising economic prospects of the new industrial towns.

New ideas, and ideals, were in the air: the right for a people to direct affairs of state through democratically elected representatives, the fairer distribution of the burden of taxation, the reform of old laws restricting ownership of property. By the 1880s, both Denmark and Sweden had witnessed the birth of modern political parties—Social Democrats, Liberals, Conservatives. In Finland, the 1906 constitution put that small, relatively backward state into the political vanguard by granting women the right to vote—the first European nation to do so.

Meanwhile, in Norway, the most pressing issue of the day was the struggle for national independence, after half a millennium of rule by its neighbouring countries. The increasingly restive, separatist Norwegians had never quite reconciled themselves to

living under the Swedish crown, and a series of relatively minor issues eventually led to a formal rupture.

The Norwegian merchant marine, for example, had become one of the world's largest: were its ships entitled to fly a Norwegian rather than a Swedish flag? And was the theoretically separate and equal kingdom of Norway entitled to establish its own consular offices wherever it chose to do so? The Swedish reply to such questions was invariably in the negative.

By 1905, Norwegian irritation had reached such a pitch that the nation's parliament—the Storting—ordained a plebescite on the question of whether to dissolve the union with Sweden. The vote was 368,211 in favour of dissolution and only 184 against it. Sweden did not demur.

After the king of Sweden had formally relinquished his second, Norwegian, crown, the Storting elected a member of the Danish royal family, Prince Carl, to the throne of Norway. In choosing to reign as Haakon VII he reached across more than 500 years of history to adopt the name of the last of the native Norse kings, Haakon VI, who had ruled Norway at the end of the 14th century.

During World War I, Norway, Denmark and Sweden remained determinedly neutral, and were thus spared the bloodshed that decimated the major belligerents. But Iceland, accustomed to running its own affairs after having been cut off from Denmark by four years of British and German blockade, afterwards insisted on becoming a sovereign state, linked to Denmark only by a common monarchy.

Meanwhile, events on the eastern front were pushing Finland towards independence. The Revolution of 1917 threw Russia into chaos, and the Finns took this opportunity to make their own bid for sovereignty.

On December 6, 1917, Finland became an independent republic, but then suffered a bloody civil war before the Bolshevik "Red" brigades, who wanted to set up a Communist government in Finland, were defeated by the Nationalist "Whites" led by General Carl Gustaf Mannerheim, a Swedo-Finnish nobleman who had served with distinction in the tsarist army.

In 1920, the Soviet government formalized relations with the newly independent Finland, recognizing a Russo-Finnish border, a part of which, in Soviet eyes, ran menacingly close to Leningrad. But fewer than 20 years elapsed before Europe again became a powder keg, giving Russia an opportunity to revise the boundary.

After Hitler and Stalin had divided up conquered Poland in 1939, at the outset of World War II, the U.S.S.R. invaded Finland with 26 to 29 divisions. To everyone's astonishment, the Soviets were repulsed by a far smaller Finnish force, consisting of only nine divisions, again led by General Mannerheim. Still, after successfully defending most of her territory in the "Winter War" of 1939–40, Finland was ultimately unable to hold out against the superior strength of her giant neighbour, and was forced to grant the Soviet Union major territorial concessions along her eastern frontiers.

Almost simultaneously, Scandinavian neutrality was breached a second time when Hitler's armies invaded both Denmark and Norway. In response, the British (subsequently to be replaced by the Americans) occupied Iceland. The Danish government capitulated almost at once to German

threats of bombing Copenhagen. The Norwegians fought a bold delaying action that was doomed to failure, because the fall of France forced the British to withdraw the expeditionary force they had sent to support them. Danes and Norwegians lived under the heel of German occupation regimes for the remainder of the war.

Sweden maintained a tenuous and rather one-sided neutrality. She kept this precarious status by allowing German troops on leave to move through her territory, and by supplying critical material for the Nazi war machine from mines and factories.

When Hitler invaded the U.S.S.R., Finland became a "co-belligerent" in an effort to win back lost territories, but after the German armies began to collapse in 1944, Finland had to change sides and become a "co-belligerent" of the Allies, fighting to expel the German troops who were making a last-ditch stand in the north of the peninsula.

In Norway, the Nazis installed a puppet government under the fascist politician Quisling—a name that was to enter the dictionary as a synonym for turncoat and traitor. His murderous police state was actively resisted by one of the toughest and most effective underground movements in Europe, directed from London by a Norwegian government-in-exile headed by the ageing but determined Haakon VII.

The king of Denmark had remained in Copenhagen, where his steadfast conduct during the war set his subjects an example of personal and passive resistance to the German occupation. For a time, Denmark as a whole seemed sufficiently obedient to qualify as Hitler's "model protectorate". But as the war progressed, the Danish resistance movement, like the Norwegian, began

to play an active part in sabotaging railway lines and communications in preparation for the Allied liberation of Europe. Among other achievements, it succeeded in saving virtually all of Denmark's Jews from Hitler's "Final Solution" by smuggling them to safety in neutral Sweden before they could be rounded up by the Germans.

During the summer of 1944, distant Iceland severed its links with Denmark by dissolving the common monarchy and declaring itself an independent republic. When peace came in 1945, Finland found itself still further reduced in size, and forced to pay massive reparations to the U.S.S.R. for its part in the war. Norway, too, had suffered heavy casualties and had lost half its merchant fleet, which was used to carry vital Allied cargoes across the Atlantic. Its two northernmost counties were virtually destroyed by the Germans' scorched earth policy, which wiped out roads, flattened buildings and returned the land to a state of near-medieval poverty and desolation.

Altogether, Scandinavia had borne more than its share of the sufferings inflicted by Hitler's war. Yet no part of Europe was quicker to recover its social and economic energies. Indeed, postwar Scandinavia was to become in many respects a model for the rest of Europe—with its democratic politics, its social conscience, its leadership in architecture and design, art and international affairs.

Again, as so often in the past, the Scandinavians were able to exercise an influence on the rest of the world that was far out of proportion to their numbers. The once unknown North was no longer the ultima Thule of civilization, but one of the most vital and creative regions in the family of nations.

SCANDINAVIA UNDER SIEGE

Finnish ski-troops, their equipment loaded on to reindeer-hauled sledges, move through Lapland during the Winter War against the U.S.S.R. in 1939–40. So silent was their approach and so expert their marksmanship that some Russians nicknamed them *Belaya Smert*—the White Death.

In September 1939, with the outbreak of World War II, the small nations of Scandinavia promptly declared their neutrality and prayed for the storm to pass them by. The well-armed Swedes were, indeed, to be spared. But for their weaker neighbours, the Finns, the Danes and the Norwegians, the days ahead were filled with anguish.

The first victims were the Finns, who woke on November 30 to find themselves under attack by the Red Army. Although the Russians themselves were still neutral at this time, they wanted to take over part of the Finnish borderland as a buffer against a possible attack by Germany. Undeterred by the massive odds against them, the Finns fought back with terrifying ferocity, inflicting 10 Soviet casualties for every one of their own.

The Finns, however, were unable to make up their losses, and in March 1940 they were forced to accept the Soviet territorial demands. But peace was to be short-lived, because in June 1941, when Hitler finally attacked the Soviet Union, the Finns joined in on the German side. In the subsequent fray, nearly three million troops saw action on Finnish soil—more than in any other Scandinavian nation.

Meanwhile, Denmark and Norway were undergoing their own ordeals. In the spring of 1940, with little warning, Hitler's forces swiftly occupied the two countries. At first, people were too stunned to react. But, as the shock of defeat wore off, defiance of the invaders increased. Unable to match the Nazi war machine on its own terms, many civilians became part-time guerrillas, ambushing German soldiers, destroying military installations and blowing up roads and railways. In the first four months of 1945 alone, the Danes carried out some 2,000 separate sabotage operations.

The price of freedom was high, and thousands of Danish and Norwegian patriots were either shot or deported. But repression merely intensified the flame of resistance—a flame that burned throughout the five dark years of the Occupation.

A German parachutist floats down to earth near Narvik in northern Norway during the Nazi assault of 1940. Hitler's war-machine demanded supplies of Swedish iron-ore; Narvik was the principal port through which it flowed to Germany.

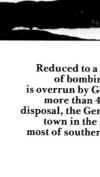

Reduced to a ruin after 30 minutes of bombing, a Norwegian town is overrun by German infantry. With more than 400 warplanes at their disposal, the Germans took town after town in the same way, occupying most of southern Norway in 25 days.

IN THE SHADOW OF THE CONQUEROR

Mingling with the crowds, two German soldiers inspect the day's catch at the fish market in occupied Copenhagen. At first, the Danes responded to their invaders with icy politeness, but by 1943, the underground had become so disruptive that the Germans declared martial law throughout the country.

Evicted from their Oslo apartment to make room for billeted German troops, a Norwegian mother and child wait as their possessions are loaded on to removal lorries. Such citizens had not only to find new accommodation, but also to go on paying the rent of the old.

A LIFE GEARED TO TWO SEASONS

Glowing above the trampled winter snow, posters advertising Mediterranean holidays line a bus shelter in Helsinki. A winter package tour to the sun is considered essential by many Scandinavians, who spend far more on vacations abroad than they earn from tourism at home.

In one of Scandinavia's favourite fairy tales—*Sampo Lappelil* "(Sampo, The Little Lapp Boy")—the King of the Trolls proclaims at midwinter that he has killed the sun and that henceforth he will rule a world of darkness and cold. His troll subjects, who are gathered in their thousands around the icy peak that serves as his throne, immediately send up a great wail of approval because, in common with all trolls, they regard the sun as being synonymous with death. According to legend, these malevolent creatures are doomed to explode into smithereens or turn into stone if they should ever be exposed to the light of the sun.

The fable could not be more artfully designed to impress upon Scandinavian children the totally alien nature of the trolls, because the trolls' reaction to the King's declaration is the exact opposite of that of humankind. In the Nordic countries, the overwhelming majority of children grow up in an environment where everyone deeply mourns the autumnal decline of the sun. For Scandinavians, sunshine is synonymous with life—something to be cherished, pursued and exploited. In winter, they seek their sun-god (Baldur, as he was known to their pagan ancestors) on the shores of the Mediterranean, the Canaries and the Azores where many apartments and hotels are owned or operated by Nordic companies. And in summer, as soon as the sun gathers strength, they take every conceivable opportunity to get out of doors and luxuriate in its warmth.

It is not so much the heat of the sun that matters to Scandinavians; more important to them is the duration of light that summer bestows, the longed-for release from winter's darkness. Each year, the lengthening nights of winter are anticipated on All Saints' Day, November 1, a public holiday recognized by northern inhabitants as the beginning of what Norwegians call *mørketiden* ("the murky time") and the Finns call *kaamosaika* ("the dark time"). In the extreme north, a period of darkness relieved only briefly by twilight has already begun. The Polar Eskimos of north-west Greenland, members of the northernmost community on earth, experience four months without sunlight, from late October to February. In mainland Scandinavia, in such northerly places as Tromsø and Hammerfest in Norway, and Utsjoki and Ivalo in Finland, the sun is below the horizon for six weeks or more from the beginning of December. And in Norway and Iceland generally, the gloom is deepened by the frequency of cloud cover. Even in the more southern cities such as Oslo, Stockholm and Helsinki, it is at least 9 a.m. before street lights are extinguished in midwinter, and they come on again at 3 p.m.

Darkness has always been a symbol of these high-latitude lands. To the inhabitants of medieval Europe, the Nordic territories were the "midnight

83

3

lands" long before the tourist industry glowingly popularized them as "lands of the midnight sun". To 17th-century Germans, Gustavus II Adolphus was *Der Löwe von Mitternach*—the lion of midnight, rather than the lion of the north. In Finland, a two or three-day old child used to be called a two or three-night child if born in midwinter.

Darkness has long haunted artistic Scandinavia, too. Cold and gloom are blamed for deaths in plays by Ibsen. They are symbols in *The House in the Dark*, a saga about the German occupation of Norway by the leading Norwegian novelist Tarje Vesaas. They are part of the powerful chiaroscuro of the Finnish poet Eino Leino, and they are inherent in the work of Swedish director Ingmar Bergman—sometimes in the very titles of his films: *Through a Glass Darkly* and *Winter Light*.

Beyond Denmark, where the climate is more closely related to that of the Netherlands and north-east Germany, the fleeting Nordic seasons of spring and autumn merge so closely with winter that it is possible to speak of a three-part winter: autumn-winter (October/November), high-winter (December/February) and spring-winter (March/April). Of the three, autumn-winter is the most depressing time of year since it offers only the promise of another prolonged period of cold and darkness ahead.

A few years ago, during *kaamosaika*, a Finnish psychiatrist, Dr. Erkki Väisänen of the University of Oulu, studied Finns living in a small northern town and found signs of increased depression and a higher incidence of alcoholism and suicide. Similarly, evidence of lower spirits was found by American journalist Edwin Kiester Jr. when he observed life in the Norwegian city of

Tromsø during *mørketiden*. He also found, much to his surprise, that the most common complaint was insomnia. "Over and over I heard the same lament. People slept fine in the summer, but, as darkness began, they couldn't fall asleep at night. When they would finally doze off, they couldn't rouse themselves in the morning." Pharmacists confirmed that prescriptions for sleeping pills increased by one third during "the murky time". And studies indicated that about a fourth of Tromsø's population of 46,000 had complaints of sleeplessness at this time, the problem being most prevalent among young adults.

The reaction to autumn-winter is much less pronounced as one moves south. Nevertheless, throughout Scandinavia, it remains the most unpopular time of year. High-winter, to be sure, brings the longest nights, but this can be darkness of a less gloomy kind. The coming of snow contributes a certain luminosity to the land; nights can have a magical quality when the full light of the moon and the stars are reflected and intensified by snow and ice. High-winter is also the time when the *aurora borealis*, the northern lights, is seen most vividly. This luminous phenomenon, caused by light emitting from the upper atmosphere as showers of sub-atomic particles from the sun pass through, takes the shape of banners or arches of light—reddish and bluish as well as white—and occurs most frequently in north Norway.

Spring-winter, too, has its drawbacks. Frozen waters become treacherous and city snow turns to brown slush. In many parts, a Scandinavian spring day will fit the description given by Norway's celebrated author Olav Duun in his novel *The Floodtide of Fate*:

"mud all over the roads and yellow-grey slush all over the fields". But whatever the conditions, at least there is always the supreme consolation that summer cannot be far behind.

There are marked variations in the severity of winter in different parts of Scandinavia. For example, temperatures of $-35°C$ are not unknown in Finnish Lapland and Swedish Norrbotten. Meanwhile, owing to the moderating effect of the Gulf Stream, it may be only $-2°C$ in Reykjavik and slightly above freezing in Bergen. Nevertheless, the fact remains that at least half of the surface area of Scandinavia is covered by snow for at least six months of the year. Average snow depths can vary greatly, from well over a metre in much of Norway, which is exposed to wet, westerly winds, to less than a fifth of a metre in parts of Finland which are sheltered by the Scandinavian mountains.

The intensity of sea-ice is similarly variable. Around the margins of Atlantic Scandinavia, it is slight; and here the saline waters of the outer ocean remain free from ice. On the other hand, every winter, for a minimum of a month or two in the south-west and for about four or five months in the north, ice forms along the thousands of kilometres of Finland's intricate coastline. And it is the same along Sweden's Bothnian coast.

On land, frost may penetrate deeply into the soil—up to a metre in the peatlands of much of Scandinavia. And, sometimes, high pressure systems build up over the continental landmass and create so-called "iron winters". Then, the entire Baltic Sea and the waters that separate Denmark and Sweden may freeze over; landscape and seascape will resemble those of the Ice Age, and ice floes may still be drifting

On Norway's Lofoten Islands, a boy
leans on a *sparkstotting*, one of three
standing idle in the snow. The "spark"
resembles a wooden chair on runners,
and is widely used in northern
Scandinavia for carrying children and
shopping through the snow.

in the Bothnian Gulf at midsummer.

The contrast between summer and winter is, for most of the Scandinavians, highly dramatic. "Winter is a certainty," wrote the Finnish author Toivo Pekkanen, "summer is an illusion." Other than flying south, there is no escaping from winter, whereas summer—illusion or not—is a season to be welcomed with almost reckless abandon. In response to these climatic extremes, two lifestyles have emerged. One is geared to combating the winter and, wherever possible, capitalizing on its few advantageous characteristics. The other is bent upon exploiting the brief summer to the maximum.

"Winter is the element for which we are born," wrote the 19th-century Finnish historian Zachris Topelius. And certainly it is still the element that has the most profound influence on the lifestyle of Scandinavians. That style, however, has changed beyond recognition since the time of Topelius, when agriculture was the primary activity and most of the family stayed indoors as much as possible during winter to conserve energy and food. Today, modern technology enables the Scandinavians to achieve victory on many fronts in their relentless war on winter's darkness and cold.

Since the coming of electricity in the late 19th century, they have increasingly challenged the darkness with an extravagance of light. Floodlighting is widely used for public buildings, neon lighting is more than generously employed for advertisements, and arc lamps seem to be twice as numerous as in other lands. Indeed, to fly over Norway, Sweden or Finland on a clear winter's night is to be aware of a surprisingly extensive pattern of lights for such thinly populated territory. Almost all Scandinavian homes—even the remotest farmsteads of Iceland—are now supplied with electricity, and many householders use it with scant regard for economy.

Scandinavians are no less extravagant with heating. The majority live in a centrally heated environment and use some degree of heating for nine months of every year. As costs of fuels steadily rise, however, every possible form of heat-conservation is practised. Double glazing has been commonly replaced by treble glazing. In some homes, metal-plated window glass serves to reflect interior heat. Thick insulating layers of glass fibre and other materials fill cavity walls and roofs; and where there are fireplaces and stoves, dampers prevent the ingress of cold air. Usually double doors are provided, even in private homes, and in many public buildings the main doors are so heavy that it is a struggle to open them.

Nevertheless, domestic heating and lighting are still a huge expense, and inevitably the costs are greatest in the least privileged areas—the thinly populated expanses of northern Sweden, Norway and Finland, and the remoter coastal settlements of Iceland. In Finland, however, there is a government heating allowance for people in high latitudes, and this is geared to the average number of days in a year—anything from 150 to 200—when the temperature falls below freezing.

Clothing is another punishment on the purse in winter. The contrast between the airless 23°C of centrally heated indoors and the sub-zero outdoors calls for heavy overcoats, furs (with the added cost of insurance and summer storage), knee-high boots, overshoes and that most dreary of footwear—galoshes. Fur hats are *de rigueur*—earflapped for military conscripts, black astrakhan for Salvation Army girls, wolfskin for dashing youths, mink for matrons and sealskin for men. Again, those who live and work in the most inclement areas incur the greatest expenditure, and the cost is so heavy that civil servants in the high latitudes are granted a winter clothing allowance.

For young and old alike, waterproof and windproof artificial fabrics and the

Brightly lit windows accentuate the darkness which shrouds Tromsø on an afternoon in early January *(left)*. On the 21st of the month—Sol Dag, or Sun Day—children in a warm schoolroom *(below)* celebrate the return of daylight with a display of paper suns.

WAGING WAR ON WINTER GLOOM

In the Norwegian town of Tromsø, 300 kilometres above the Arctic Circle, the sun sets on November 25 and does not reappear for nearly two months. During this dark time, the town's 46,000 inhabitants fight depression by keeping their houses brightly lit and leading a gregarious life: an average Tromsø family uses 20 per cent more electricity than one in the south of the country, and there are more restaurant seats per head than in any other Norwegian town.

The ordeal ends at last on January 21 when the sun briefly rises again, bringing four minutes of daylight and a welcome release from gloom.

3

humble zip have greatly helped the winter wardrobe. Nevertheless, winter wear imposes a variety of problems and demands. Since winter is very much the season for entertaining at home, even the most modest apartment will have a built-in cupboard immediately adjacent to the entrance to receive the clutter of coats, overshoes and shoe-bags. Theatres and concert halls have armies of well-trained cloakroom attendants. Restaurants usually have a fixed charge for accommodating winter clothing in their cloakrooms. And doing your winter shopping in a super-heated supermarket can be an extremely sweaty business.

Various other costs and chores are necessitated by the winter cold. Householders with gardens need to protect their roses, shrubs and other less hardy plants in wrappings of straw, sacking or paper. Except in the more favoured areas, such as Denmark and the western coastlands of Norway and Sweden, lawns will require re-seeding after the thaw. Down by the water's edge, millions of pleasure-boats must be provided with winter accommodation. The majority of motorists need to fit their cars with a second set of heavy-service tyres to reduce the risk of skidding on icy roads, and in most modern residences the car is treated to a centrally heated garage.

At the national level, the cost of fighting winter can be astronomical. It is estimated that the war on winter consumes at least 5 per cent of Finland's gross domestic product. No one can afford to gamble on a mild winter; all investment is in anticipation of severe conditions. Road, railway and airport maintenance calls for snow ploughs, snow blowers, point heaters, snow fences and (in Norway) hundreds of

kilometres of snow sheds to protect mountain railway tracks from drifts and avalanches. Norway has by far the greatest problem with snow accumulation. As recently as a generation ago, there was rarely continuous road communication between east and west Norway in the winter. Today, only one major route is likely to be kept open during a hard winter—the main highway across the Hardangervidda, linking Oslo and Bergen.

Of the Scandinavian countries, excluding Denmark, Finland is the least affected by snow. Nevertheless, its central road authority musters some 1,600 snow ploughs and maintains some 3,500 kilometres of snow fences to prevent drifting across road surfaces. In towns, snow clearance keeps an army of labourers busy. In Helsinki, emergency clearance may be undertaken by local smallholders using their own tractors and trailers to cart snow to one of the city's mountainous snow dumps. Caretakers, lashed to chimney stacks

and other structures for safety, clamber over rooftops to clear them of snow before avalanches descend on passing pedestrians. But it is impossible to keep roads and pavements free of ice, and every year in Helsinki alone hundreds of people suffer broken bones.

Such weather conditions impose great restraints on any outdoor activity (the construction industry is especially vulnerable) and make for seasonal un- and under-employment. The labour problem is met by unemployment relief, by insurance payments and by the subsidization of construction activity to offset the extra costs of continuous winter work. In some cases, continuity can be maintained by providing a heated environment. In towns of central Finland and north Sweden, office blocks, apartments or public buildings under construction may be wrapped in plastic, while hot-air blowers boost the inside temperature to allow work with concrete, cement and brick-laying. Some work-sites are covered permanently, among them one of Wärtsila's shipyards in Helsinki, which embraces a dock capable of accommodating vessels of more than 20,000 tonnes.

There can be no such protection for forest workers. The felling of conifers is always confined to periods when snow is on the ground to facilitate haulage. Inevitably, at such times, low temperatures and blizzards frequently interrupt schedules. But at least working conditions have been greatly eased by mechanization—the motor saw, tractors, and mechanical loading and log-bundling. In pre-war years, after the first heavy falls of snow, lumberjacks in their tens of thousands migrated with their horses to the woodlands of north Sweden and Finland. Then, for four or five months, they lived in fairly primitive conditions, based in huge communal huts and trekking increasingly great distances to work as they cleared the nearest forest. Today, as a result of mechanized harvesting, far fewer men are needed, and mobile caravans are used to reduce the number of journeys to and from the working area. Moreover, amenities at the base camps are now rigorously controlled by state legislation. Buildings must conform to precise standards. There are domestic staff to provide meals. Hygiene is strictly monitored, and to reduce the risk of brawling, alcohol is banned.

Winter presents a greater challenge for those who earn their living at sea. Until the coming of steel-plated steamships in the late 19th century, most Scandinavian vessels were laid up for six months, and Iceland suffered a break in communications for several months on end. Storms and gales regularly caused disasters. Not surprisingly, the legend of the *Flying Dutchman* had its setting in the skerries of western Norway. And one of Europe's most notorious graveyards of shipping is sited off the Danish Skaw, where the masts and bulkheads of wrecked vessels still testify to hundreds of tragedies. Indeed, one of the reasons for the construction in the 1890s of the Kiel Canal, cutting across the neck of the Jutland peninsula in north Germany, was to provide a sheltered route for shipping to pass from the North Sea through to the Baltic Sea.

It is little more than a century since Sweden made the first tentative efforts to maintain continuous winter communication with Finland and the island of Gotland by way of steam packets. In the early 1890s, the first crude antecedents of the modern icebreakers were introduced. Now Finland has a fleet of about 10 major icebreakers, supplemented by a number of smaller vessels which clear ice in and around the major harbours. Sweden has seven icebreakers and Denmark four; however, since 1961, there has been a formal agreement for co-operation in the employment of icebreaker fleets between Norway, Denmark, Sweden and Finland. The Finnish icebreaker fleet also co-operates with Russian icebreakers in the Gulf of Finland.

The strategy of Finland and Sweden is to concentrate icebreaker operations initially in the Gulf of Bothnia. But here the battle is often lost. The northern Bothnian ports, such as Luleå, Kemi and Oulu, are liable to be closed for four months, from early January onwards. When this happens, the icebreaker fleet moves south and devotes most of its labours to keeping open the channels for the shipping that uses the leading export harbours of Kotka, Hamina, Rauma, Turku and Helsinki. On the Swedish side of the Bothnian Sea, ports south of Umeå are not normally affected by icing to a serious degree. As the thaw sets in, the fleet can transfer its efforts to hastening the re-opening of the northern Bothnian ports.

In severe winters, it is still possible for ferries to be trapped in the ice of the central Baltic, and even icebreakers themselves may have the greatest difficulty in keeping on the move. The most critical time of year is late February to late March; then, icebreaker crews— each numbering about 40 men, plus a few women who are employed in the catering service—may work for two or three weeks without a break. Technically, icebreakers could maintain continuity of shipping to all Finnish and Swedish harbours. However, this is not attempted because it is cheaper either to export to the nearest open harbour or to stockpile goods before the big freeze sets in.

In addition to icebreakers, ice-forecasting has become a key aid to Scandinavian shipping in winter. Finland and Sweden have been accumulating evidence of the behaviour of ice in the Baltic basin for well over half a century; indeed, in the 1930s, Finland prepared the first ice atlas of the Baltic, complete with its own vocabulary of ice types and forms. Now it is possible to make predictions of ice formation and movement based on clearly identifiable weather patterns. Wind direction is particularly important once ice has begun to form. For example, the prevailing westerly winds cause ice floes to drift away from the Swedish coast and to form pack ice along the Finnish shores. Weekly ice charts are produced for all of the Baltic area and daily situation reports are provided for the approaches to the principal harbours. Formerly, they were compiled from the reports of icebreakers, merchant and naval ships, aircraft and lighthouses. Today, satellite photography is a principal source of information.

While Finnish and Swedish ports on the Gulf of Bothnia may be closed by ice for months, Norwegian ships are able to operate throughout winter on the western side of mainland Scandinavia. Indeed, for at least a millennium, between February and April each year, fishermen have reaped an extraordinary cod harvest in ice-free Vestfjord, on the north-west coast of Norway. Vestfjord is protected on its north and west sides by the 150-kilometre-long wall of the Lofoten Islands, whose jagged peaks soar upwards like the spines of a gigantic dragon's back; and here, warmer waters of the Gulf Stream mingle with

3

the cooler waters of Arctic Norway to produce outstanding conditions for the production of plankton, the myriad tiny creatures that are the principal food of the cod.

Ten centuries ago, on a visit to Alfred, King of Wessex in England, the north Norwegian trader Othere made the first recorded report of the fishing bonanza at this supreme cod feeding-ground. Today, the spectacle is still astonishing: vessels of all shapes, sizes and colours bob on the water for as far as the eye can see, all set against a dramatic backcloth of snow-clad pinnacles. Ashore, fish are beheaded and gutted and hung on fish racks to dry, or filleted and frozen for the international market. Fish meal and cod-liver oil factories belch out their unsavoury odours, and down in the harbours a vast company of followers afloat await the return of the fishing fleet: hospital ships, generator ships, Salvation Army ships, tourist ships and entertainment ships, some of which even carry all the paraphernalia of a travelling circus. With some justification, the annual Lofoten harvest has been called "the greatest fishing show on earth".

Winter gives a certain grim earnestness to daily life in the greater part of Scandinavia, but at the same time it yields its own distinct forms of relaxation and enjoyment. Winter is the season when social life reaches a climax. As soon as people have cast off the melancholy of autumn, they plunge into the traditional round of parties, visits to friends, and outings to the plays and concerts that are staged in even the smallest towns. For Norwegians, Swedes and Finns, it is a time when winter sports facilities are available on virtually every doorstep. It is a time, too, of numerous festivals and anniversary days.

On Father's Day (the second Sunday in November), candles appear on graves all over Finland, and they illuminate all war cemeteries on Independence Day (December 6). In Sweden, the festival season starts on December 13, St. Lucia's Day, when throughout the land, white-robed Lucias wear crowns with circlets of lighted candles. Then, accompanied by candle-bearing attendants and boys carrying starred wands, they sing in a procession on their way with coffee and cakes to the elders of countless households. Candles are also invariably lit when guests are entertained for a meal. And, of course, in anticipation of Yuletide (*Jul* is the old Scandinavian word for the Christmas season), candlelit or electric-lit fir trees spring up in every street and home. Most Danish homes also display a wreath of pine twigs decorated with four candles, and over all of Scandinavia, at social gatherings, homes are further illuminated when aquavit is set aflame on top of the mulled wine, so providing a beverage with the warming name of *glögg*.

It seems natural that these lands of Christmas trees and reindeer should have become the presumed home of Father Christmas. Yet Santa Claus is essentially an importation so far as Scandinavians are concerned. Their own native Christmastide visitor is the *nisse* or gnome—a good-humoured household sprite with short legs, a long-flowing beard and red-tasselled cap, who is reckoned to be several thousands of years old. Fifty years ago he was rarely seen, though he might be lured to the doorstep by a bowl of porridge put out on Christmas Eve. Today in Iceland, the first *nisser* are supposed to arrive 13 days before Christmas and remain until the first week of the New Year. Elsewhere in Scandinavia, *nisser* seem to have lost their shyness and to have yielded to the temptations of the commercial world. They appear on the streets carrying billboards and haunt the department stores, especially in the toy sections.

Despite his foreign origins, Santa Claus is now an established Scandinavian institution, and there are children worldwide who locate his home in the capital of Finnish Lapland, Rovaniemi, a city of 30,000 people in which the postal authorities have generously accepted the responsibility of answering post addressed to him. Alternatively, some children locate his home in Greenland or Iceland. And, not to be outdone, an American entrepreneur has sensed profit in a Santaland, a Disney-style tourist complex comprising the home and workshops of Father Christmas, as well as such garish attractions as a Palace of the Snow Queen and a Dinosaur Park. Despite much opposition, it has been created in Gesunda, a village of 300 souls overlooking Siljan, one of Sweden's most beautiful lakes, in the holiday area of Dalarna.

By the time of the Christmas holiday, the most welcome bonus of the long winter is being enjoyed: the three or four-month skiing season. In Norway, Sweden and Finland, most citizens can enjoy virtually unimpeded cross-country skiing from their street corner, if not from their doorstep. In the words of a suburban Stockholmer, "There is nothing to stop you skiing from here to Lapland." Children are put on skis as soon as they can walk and, as the late President Kekkonen of Finland demonstrated, some devotees continue skiing into their eighties or more. In Finland alone, more than a

Standing on a beam, a fishery worker hangs cod slit lengthwise on a rack to dry—a simple method of preserving. Traditional drying racks are declining in number due to the increasing use of refrigeration, but are still used on the Lofoten Islands *(below)*, one of the richest breeding-grounds for cod.

3

On the edge of Norway's Jostedalsbre glacier, summer skiers file over matting, which protects their skis from the rough ground between snowfields. The country's mountainous western region has several resorts from which skiing is possible all the year round.

million skiers—fully a quarter of the total population—are in possession of proficiency certificates issued by the national skiing society, recognizing that they have mastered the basic arts of the sport. There are skiing competitions in innumerable Finnish, Norwegian and Swedish towns, and ski-jumps are provided by the thousand.

This winter bonus originated long ago. Ski-type wooden runners, dated by carbon analysis as being six to seven thousand years old, have been recovered from bogs in Sweden and Finland, and from the surface of a Norwegian glacier. But it is impossible to tell how effectively they were used. Indeed, high-speed, competitive skiing—as we know it today—did not begin until the mid-19th century when Sondre Norheim, a farmer from the district of Telemark, introduced a stiff binding around the heel, fastening the foot to the ski in much the same way as a skate, and so making it possible to turn and jump. Previously, for thousands of years, skiers had used only a toe-strap, which gave little manoeuvrability.

As a result of heel-binding, the slalom and jumping developed rapidly. In the 1880s, skiing competitions began almost simultaneously in Sweden, Finland and Norway; and from the beginning, there were women participants in the events. A.E. Nordenskiöld, the scientist and arctic explorer who led the first expedition through the North-East Passage, is usually credited with the foundation of official skiing contests in Sweden in 1884. One of his ardent admirers, Fridtjof Nansen, the first man to cross Greenland on skis, did much to popularize the sport in his native Norway.

Today, the skiing season has a number of climaxes. In the Swedish re-

gion of Dalarna, on the first Sunday in March, thousands participate in the 90-kilometre Vasa race, which commemorates the occasion in 1521 when men from Dalarna skied to Norway to ask Gustavus Vasa, the future king of Sweden, to return as their leader. In Norway, the competitions staged at Holmenkollen's sky-high ski-jump gain worldwide television coverage, and every year large crowds gather to watch the major events of the Finnish winter sporting calendar at Lahti. Schools usually enjoy skiing holidays in February; and when Easter falls early in the year, almost all active Norwegians take to the slopes for the last great holiday of the winter season. As spring approaches, enthusiasts follow the ski-

ing northwards, to the fells of Lapland. And even in summer the action continues. Dedicated skiers travel to the snowfields of western Norway's largest glacier, 815-square kilometre Jostedalsbre, for the competitions in July. Others, aiming to keep their muscles in trim, embark upon wheeled skis, thrusting themselves along footpaths and country roads.

Ice provides a setting for other winter activities, but it no longer rivals snow. Now that most people can afford high-class ski equipment, ice-skating does not attract quite such a following as it had in the 1930s, in the heyday of Norway's Sonja Henie. At that time, it was the great Scandinavian dream to emulate the success of the incompara-

One of Finland's thousands of dedicated skiers keeps in summer trim with the aid of wheeled skis on a forest road. Over 100 annual cross-country treks and marathons, each attracting up to 4,000 entrants, encourage a competitive attitude to skiing.

ble Oslo girl who became world figure-skating champion at the age of 13, retained the title for 10 successive years, won three Olympic championships, then emigrated to Hollywood to become a multimillion-dollar film star.

Ice-hockey, however, is increasingly popular in Norway, Sweden and Finland, and winter trotting races on ice-covered lakes have become a regular country sport. Ice-yachting, which originated in the early 17th century, still retains a following. And, for the more sedentary, ice-hole fishing is as popular as ever. Only the approach to this activity has changed. The traditional ice-hole fisherman was hoping to catch something to eat. His modern counter-part—replete with tent, protective clothing, heater and a little warming alcohol—is simply enjoying a hobby. In Finland, a national ice-hole fishing

competition attracts as many as 5,000 competitors every year.

Autumn-winter is the main hunting season in the north, where elk have become the principal quarry. Their sheer numbers, together with the damage they cause to growing timber and the danger they present to motorists, have made them something of a menace in Sweden and Finland. Consequently, every year more than 70,000 licences to kill them are issued in Finland, and many more in Sweden.

In Lapland, wolf packs—some of them intruding from the vast forests of the Soviet Union—can be a threat to the domesticated reindeer. They are pursued by helicopter as well as by hunters on skis. Winter seal-hunting, once a significant seasonal activity in the Bothnian islands, also continues, but now only in the Vaasa archipelago.

It is estimated that there are some 20,000 seals in these waters, and they are the principal predators upon the valuable salmon. They are pursued in traditional style by white-camouflaged hunters who move on skis, dragging sleighs on which to carry their quarry back to the mainland.

Scandinavia's hunting season comes to an end with the arrival of spring-winter and the long, gradual thaw. In late April, in the woodlands of Sweden and Finland, the sky-blue *Anemone hepatica* and the first mouse-eared birch leaves are the harbingers of the new season. Among the oak and beech woods of Denmark, the bluebells are in bloom. In general, however, the Scandinavian spring is noted more for bringing disruption than visual attractions. In Norway, Sweden and Finland, the awesome thunder of *islossning*—the

CELEBRATIONS OF MIDSUMMER

On Lake Siljan, in the Swedish region of Dalarna, a traditional "church boat" carries women in local dress to a midsummer service. Two fiddlers sit in the boat's bow, while the pastor waves from the stern.

In lands of winter darkness, there is special reason to celebrate the longest day of summer. Throughout all of Scandinavia, Midsummer's Eve is marked, as it has been for centuries, by music, merry-making and the wearing of festive clothes. The style in the cities is to carouse at open-air entertainments or all-night parties which stretch through the brief twilight hours. In the country, however, the more traditional festivities are still popular. In Sweden, and particularly in the folklore-minded region of Dalarna, the revels focus on gaily decorated maypoles around which dancers pass in rings. In Finland, sausages are grilled on bonfires lit to brighten the brief summer night.

94

Wearing wide-screen shades against the sun, four young girls in a Stockholm street celebrate midsummer with good-humoured improvisation. Garlands of leaves and flowers are their sole gesture to tradition.

On one of the islands in the Stockholm archipelago, children and parents prepare to dance around a maypole to the music of a violin and an accordion. Maypoles are never erected before the eve of Midsummer's Day, which is always celebrated in Sweden on the Saturday nearest to June 24.

3

break-up of river ice—warns people of imminent floods. In the mountains of Norway, destructive avalanches are generated by melting snow. In Iceland, boulders released by the thaw rattle down the scree slopes on to farmlands. In the northern cities, snow melts by day and becomes ribbed ice by night. On lakes and bays, winter roads marked out by stakes literally melt away, and in the archipelagos along the Bothnian Sea, they declare that spring has properly arrived in late March or early April when the first lorry or car plunges through the ice.

Even then, spring remains essentially a wintry season. Huge expenditure on repairs is incurred as frost plays havoc with the foundations of roads and airfields. And on May Day, a public holiday when matriculating university students traditionally don their white caps and radicals parade with red banners, the weather is still cold enough for overcoats to be worn in the greater part of Scandinavia, and the majority of trees remain bare of leaves. Only now does winter at last begin to retreat to the fells, where it lingers in the countless deep-frozen swamps and bogs.

Given such a long and constraining winter, it is natural that the Scandinavian summer should be a cause of rhapsody. August Strindberg saw it as a season when "in all the countries of the North, the earth is a bride and the ground is full of gladness". For the Danish author, Johannes V. Jensen, it was "all sunshine, velvet and south wind". Of course, summer temperatures vary considerably over such a vast area, from a July mean of 11°C in Reykjavik to 17°C in Copenhagen, and over much of the land unseasonal frosts can still strike. But everywhere, dark-ness gives way to longed-for light. Those who live within the Arctic Circle experience the nightless days of the midnight sun. Elsewhere, there are several weeks when twilight continues through the small hours, creating the so-called "white nights" around mid-summer that are recognized as the most romantic time of year.

The responsive vegetational surge that heralds the coming of summer has to be seen to be believed. It seems almost possible to hear the plants growing. And the perfume of flowers is also unforgettable. The scent of lilac in the hedges and lily-of-the-valley in the woodlands were balm to the tormented Strindberg, as recorded in his *Diary of a Madman*. The Finnish poet Katri Vala has written about "the pagan smell of earth's skin", as yielded by the millions of hectares of birches breaking into leaf and by conifers that are warmed by day and cooled by night. Icelanders know that summer has arrived when the marsh marigold and the globe flower bloom, and when cotton grass clads the swamps with a white mantle.

The great flocks of returning birds —the earliest blown in on western winds in April—is equally remarkable. Some species, to be sure, have become fewer in number than they were in the past. For example, the once ubiquitous stork, with its twiggy nests on Jutland housetops and its beak-clapping young, finds less to feed on now that Denmark's farmers have reclaimed most of the peat bogs and drained the salt marshes where it used to flourish. But seabirds are undiminished in number. Above all, they crowd the cliffs of Iceland, the Faeroe Islands and north Norway, and they thrive on the rich marine life of the coastal waters. Water fowl take possession of the lakes. Wild geese honk their way to high latitudes. And after a week of warmth, midges and mosquitoes breed in clouds—to the gratification of swift and swallow, but much to the discomfiture of reindeer.

The arrival of summer is accompanied by mass movement on the land. Partly to avoid the affliction of insects, domesticated herds of reindeer migrate to high altitudes or to the coastal pastures of Norway's northern seaboard. In the Baltic archipelagos, cattle are still ferried across to traditional grazing grounds on the many uninhabited islands. In south-west Norway, sheep are transported from the grasslands of the promontory of Jaeren to highland pastures as much as 50 to 60 kilometres away. In Iceland, there is what Halldor Laxness, the Nobel novelist, has called "a marathon of thousands of sheep" moving to "the sweets of the wilderness". In addition, wild animals emerge from winter hibernation—most notably the bear, now a protected species, who roams the backwoods of Finland and north Sweden.

By June, summer has cast its spell upon Scandinavia at large. Towns, parks, gardens and railway stations are riotously red as their geraniums, petunias, salvias and cannas respond to the intense and prolonged light. Purple heather cloaks the heathlands of Jutland. The island of Gotland is distinguished by an extraordinary range of blue-flowering plants: chicory, veronicas, campanulas, pansies and the precious *Anemone pulsatilla*, used as motifs on the island's tourist souvenirs. And best of all, innumerable flowers mantle the oak and hazel glades around the margins of the Swedish and Finnish archipelagos—the "peasants' parks", as they were named by Sweden's great botanist, Carl Linnaeus.

The time of flowers yields to the time of fruits. Orchards and soft fruits are abundant in the principal Danish islands. Further north, in Norway's Sognefjord, the raspberries—shipped by the bucketful to preserving factories—are arguably the fattest, and certainly the best flavoured, in the world. The wild berry crop, too, is generous—strawberry, raspberry, gooseberry, currant, cowberry, bilberry, whortleberry, blueberry, cloudberry, rowanberry and seathorn berry. In addition there is the exotic *Rubus arcticus*, or Arctic strawberry, a berry unique to parts of Finland and Soviet Karelia, which is now an endangered species.

"My land is strawberry land: the stranger's land is bilberry land," runs a Finnish proverb, and as if to emphasize the point, the village of Suonenjoki in central Finland has its own nationally famous strawberry festival. But there the strawberries are cultivated, in contrast to the wild strawberries hallowed in the film of that name by Ingmar Bergman. In fact, the Swedish metaphor for a particularly delectable spot is *smultronställe*, a wild strawberry place. Hence, Dag Hammarskjold, the late Swedish Secretary General of the United Nations, who was also something of a poet, summed up the essence of summer in these lines:

Midges dancing—like smoke from a furnace.
A slow-worm asleep on the footpath
To the wild strawberry place.

Just as the war on darkness and cold has imposed a distinct winter lifestyle on Scandinavians, so a passion for sunshine—and for the open-air—has greatly influenced the style and rhythm of their life in summer. Most notably, it has led to the creation of a two-house

Ornate wooden summer houses—one of which *(top)* is now preserved as a museum—adorn "colony gardens" in the Copenhagen suburbs. Plots in the gardens can be bought or rented by flat-dwellers, providing a welcome escape from inner-city life and the chance to cultivate a small plot of land.

society. The majority of Scandinavian families now have access to a second residence in the country, which may be an elaborate villa or hunting lodge, or a simple hut built of logs or assembled from a pre-fabricated kit; and most commonly, the homes are sited near water to allow fishing or boating. (There are a quarter of a million leisure boats in Norway alone, almost one for every two families.)

In turn, a passion for sunshine has also spurred the demand for a generous holiday allowance. On average, Scandinavian workers have five weeks' holiday a year. Moreover, schoolchildren in all five countries have almost three full months of holiday in summer, from late May to late August, and it is not unusual for mothers and children to spend the whole period at their home in the country, perhaps being joined by fathers at weekends.

Meanwhile, city work continues, but at summer's own leisurely pace. Office hours—now starting at least as early as 8 a.m. and finishing not later than 3 p.m.—are brought forward to allow workers to take maximum advantage of the long, light days. And to prevent any sunshine being squandered, most of the workers opt for an alfresco sandwich lunch.

At the approach of Midsummer's Day in late June, the great exodus from the cities begins. From now until the end of August, the chances of completing a significant business transaction are fairly negligible. Large companies operate with skeleton staffs, because the great mass of their employees, as though responding to some primeval call of the wild, relinquish their town life for a grass-roots existence of informality bordering on downright primitivism. In the words of the Danish

3

novelist Martin A. Hansen, the Scandinavian summer is "a time of liberation through nature."

Nature is the key word. Whether the second "holiday" homes are near sea, lake or river, in a forest or on an island, they are essentially in natural surroundings where a simplified lifestyle may be enjoyed far away from the madding crowd. To be sure, some families will take along a wealth of modern gadgets: propane cookers, refrigerators, portable television, hi-fi and perhaps even a radio telephone. But many others stay in homes without electricity and main services, and so far removed from civilization that only an extended journey by car or boat enables them to acquire provisions from the nearest general shop.

Another popular form of escape for urbanites is the *kolonigaard* ("colony garden"), a plot of arable land sited on the outskirts of town. These gardens—rented and tended by tens of thousands of Scandinavians—were originally established in Denmark in the late 19th century. Nowadays, the average "colony garden" measures about a quarter of a hectare—a neatly maintained plot with trim surrounding hedges, fruit trees, vegetables, greenhouses and, very often, a small wooden hut for weekend habitation.

In addition to escaping to their country homes or gardens, many Scandinavians like to explore the great wilderness areas of their homelands. Many of these have been incorporated in the national parks that have burgeoned during the last generation. Norway, Sweden and Iceland all have more than half a million hectares reserved as national parks; Sweden also boasts nearly a million hectares of protected nature reserves. Finland has a huge conservation area focused on its south-western archipelago. And in con-

Aided by relatives, a farmer harvests raspberries from his holding beside the spectacular Sognefjord in Norway. Soft fruit has grown along the sheltered shores of the fjord since the Middle Ages, but modern transport was needed to make it commercially viable.

In the peaceful light of a summer's
evening, fishermen try their luck on
one of the tributaries of the Sognefjord.
At least a quarter of the Norwegian
population are keen anglers, and
virtually every child will have his or
her own rod.

3

servation-minded Denmark, where the pressures on a limited land area are so much greater, there are 75 wildlife reserves and about 14,000 hectares of state forest reserves.

Other European countries possess great nature reserves. But it is the general freedom and ease of access to the countryside that so strongly distinguishes this part of the world in summer. Camping grounds and caravan sites abound throughout the Nordic countries. In the fells of Norway, Sweden and north Finland, old-established overnight huts are stationed at intervals along well-marked hiking trails. Be it on the broad beaches and sheltered dunes of Jutland, the pony trails of Iceland, or the totally barren and icy wastes of the east coast of Greenland (to which there are daily flights from Reykjavik), every Scandinavian can, in his or her own way, seek "liberation through nature".

Such widespread access to the land is complemented by access to the water. The majority of Scandinavians live within easy reach of lakes, rivers or the sea; therefore, aquatic sports—yachting, water-skiing, windsurfing and swimming—are especially popular in the summertime. None is more prevalent than fishing. It is true that some of Norway's salmon rivers have been leased for several generations to affluent foreigners; however, for the most part, fishing amenities are open to all, and the amateur fisherman far outnumbers his professional counterpart in all the Nordic countries.

Nets and traps are set daily in the shallow waters near countless summer cottages; and rods and lines are stored in almost every home. Perch and pike are the principal lake fish. In the eastern interior of Finland, the lakes also offer the delicate little *muikku*, a diminutive member of the trout family and the basis for *kalakukko*, the fish pie that is the region's speciality. Of river fish, the most common—depending on the area—are salmon, trout and white fish or lavaret. Traditionally, the lavaret is smoked, whereas the salmon is more commonly salted and eaten raw.

Besides exploring their own countryside, Scandinavians also flock to the crowded tourist attractions of each other's countries. They may be drawn to the icy caverns of Norway's ancient silver mines at Kongsberg or the forestry museum beside the rushing waters of Norway's biggest river, the Laagen; to the humble surroundings of Hans Christian Andersen's birthplace in Odense or the splendours of the royal castle of Frederiksborg; to the serenities of Mårbacka, home of Sweden's foremost authoress, Selma Lagerlöf, or the picturesque retreat of the Swedish artist Anders Zorn on Lake Siljan; to Marshal Mannerheim's modest manorial birthplace at Louhisaari or the apotheosis of domestic architecture in Finland—Eliel Saarinen's home at Vitträsk near Helsinki. Increasing numbers, too, make the pilgrimage to see Iceland's Thingvellir, the site of the nation's original parliament.

Summer is also a time of wide-ranging cultural activity. Chamber concerts bring to life Edvard Grieg's home at Troldhaugen; intimate opera performed in Gustavus III's rococo theatre at Drottningholm conjures up memories of the Swedish singer, Jenny Lind. Operas of a new generation of Finnish composers, such as Aulis Salonen and Joonas Kokkonen, are heard in the gaunt castle of Savonlinna; Hamlet reappears regularly at Elsinore; and Norway's battle between heathen and Christian is often re-enacted at Sticklestad, where St. Olav met his death in 1030.

Another great attraction—for both Scandinavians and overseas tourists alike—is the extraordinary open-air theatre of Tampere in Finland. Here, the entire auditorium—an 800-seater shell-shaped bowl—rotates to present changes of scene for the popular productions of Väinö Linna's famous epic of the Winter War, *The Unknown Soldier*. Elsewhere, open-air theatres spring up like mushrooms (there are reputed to be 200 in Finland alone) and almost every district sets up its own music or folk festival, at which traditional instruments such as the Hardanger fiddle of Norway or the harp-like *kantele* of Finland can be heard. And, of course, from the end of May until the beginning of September, there is Copenhagen's Tivoli Gardens, which can still be aptly described, in the words of the 19th-century Scandinavophile Edmund Gosse, as "the most blameless place of summer entertainment in the whole of northern Europe".

Each of the Nordic countries has its own distinct summer diversions. However, one spectacular and supremely joyful occasion is shared by all Scandinavians: the celebration of Midsummer's Eve, relic of a pagan festival that honoured the longest day, but is now dedicated to the name of St. John the Baptist, more popularly known as St. Hans. On this liveliest night of the year, bonfires blaze splendidly beside lakes and on seashores; fireworks are let off in the dusk that precedes the dawn. Everywhere there are barbecued meals and more alcohol is consumed than at any other time of the year—an excess partly explained by the fact that midsummer is invariably the time

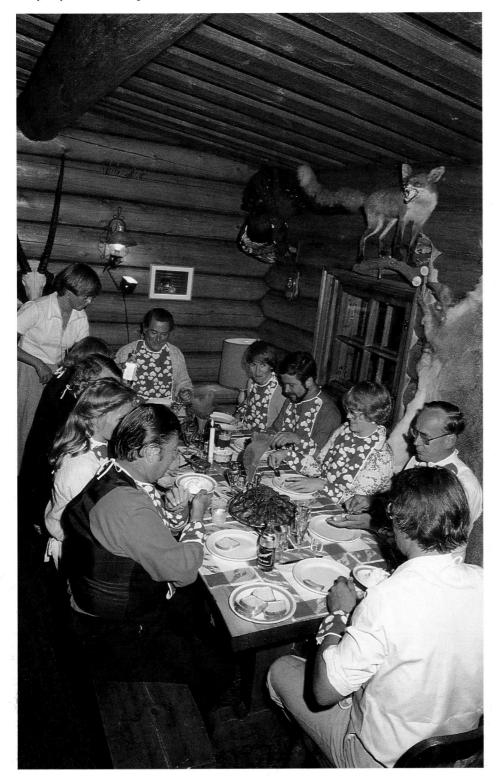

A Finnish restaurant party wearing protective bibs and cuffs prepares to attack a pile of crayfish, usually eaten in August. A crayfish feast is a messy but convivial affair, traditional to both Finns and Swedes. Due to overfishing, many crayfish are now imported.

when unemployment is at its lowest and spending power at its highest.

Once upon time, it was the custom for young ladies to place seven different wild flowers under their pillow on Midsummer's Eve in order to encourage dreams about the man they would marry. Nowadays, few young ladies get their heads upon a pillow before this night of revelry has passed. But some traditions still survive. Celebrations still include old-fashioned "ring dances", which involve all the company joining hands and, accompanied by concertinas, singing as they circle around the embers of the bonfire. Then, again, over much of Scandinavia, the maypole—named not after the month of May but derived from the Old Norse verb *maja*, to adorn—remains the colourful symbol of midsummer.

Maypoles are most spectacular in the Åland Islands, where they commonly stand as tall as masts, garlanded with leaves and flowers, and crowned with ships, weathercocks, windmills and flags. Here, they are left standing for as long as possible. However, they have already become tattered by the middle of August when Scandinavians begin holding their colourful crayfish parties. At these traditional feasts, unique to Nordic countries, mounds of the delectable little red crustaceans glow in the light of lanterns as redbibbed, sun-tanned guests chase down each tail with a glass of aquavit. It is the last crayfish party—not the last rose of summer—that causes nostalgia. By then, September has arrived—time for summer homes to be shuttered against autumn gales and for the nature-lovers of Scandinavia to return to their dust-sheeted town flats and the gloomy prospect of facing another long, sun-starved winter.

LIVING IN WINTER'S ICY GRIP

Every year, the primeval forces of winter close in upon the Scandinavian countries, but they no longer bring the restraints nor the real threat to survival that for centuries they inflicted upon a large part of the population. Modern technology has provided so many means of combating the effects of the cold season that the people of the far north are able to control their environment to a far greater degree.

Half a century ago, most Scandinavians were engaged in farming, forestry, fishing or mining, and the rhythm of the seasons largely controlled their activity. A short summer of intense labour for all the family contrasted with the relative passivity and confinement of winter. Since then, industrialization has significantly reduced seasonal unemployment; and more scientific agricultural methods have led to food surpluses, so removing the spectre of winter privation. Importantly, too, communications are no longer disrupted by snow and ice. Workers can be confident of reaching their factories and offices, and children are driven to school on time by bus.

Instead of being imprisoned by winter conditions, Scandinavians can now enjoy them. Just as urban inhabitants escape to their country retreats at every available opportunity in summer, so they take with equal gusto to frozen lakes and snow-covered slopes. Winter sports are nowhere more popular than among the people of north Scandinavia. Snow and ice-borne activities have proliferated to fill increased leisure time; in the process, a number of traditional skills, developed as an aid to winter survival, have reappeared strictly as amusements. Every winter, for example, tens of thousands of Scandinavians compete at ice-hole fishing, once a vital means of obtaining winter protein. Similarly, ice-sailing boats, introduced centuries ago as emergency winter transport, are now used strictly for pleasure.

Children romp in an icy school playground in the Norwegian city of Trondheim. Although the duration of snow cover around Trondheimfjord itself is relatively short-lived, the greater part of the country is blanketed for more than 180 days a year.

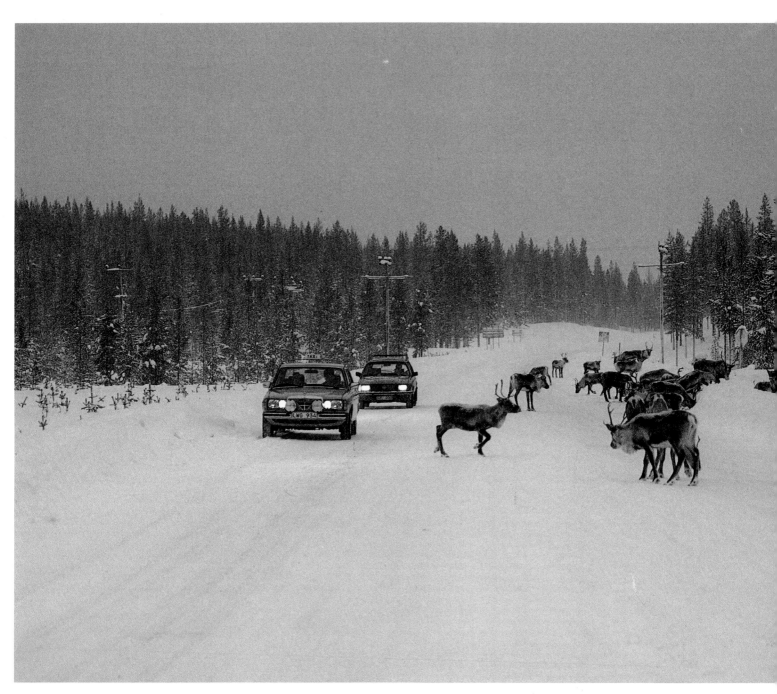

Cars on a snow-ploughed road in Swedish Lapland skirt gingerly past loitering reindeer. Free-roaming deer and elk cause many accidents each year, and the Lapps, who own Sweden's 250,000 domesticated reindeer, receive government compensation for animals killed.

104

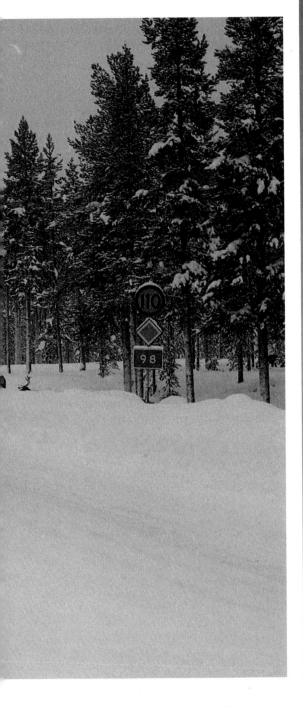

In Nordkalotten, close by the Norwegian–Swedish border, wind-driven snow encrusts a road sign. Efficient snow-clearing services keep all of Arctic Scandinavia's main roads and runways clear throughout winter.

A homesteader in a remote corner of the Swedish backwoods—one of the few areas to fall outside the range of the national electrical grid—cuts wood for fuel. Despite no electricity, he has such conveniences as a petrol-driven saw, a van, and a telephone to keep in touch with the outside world.

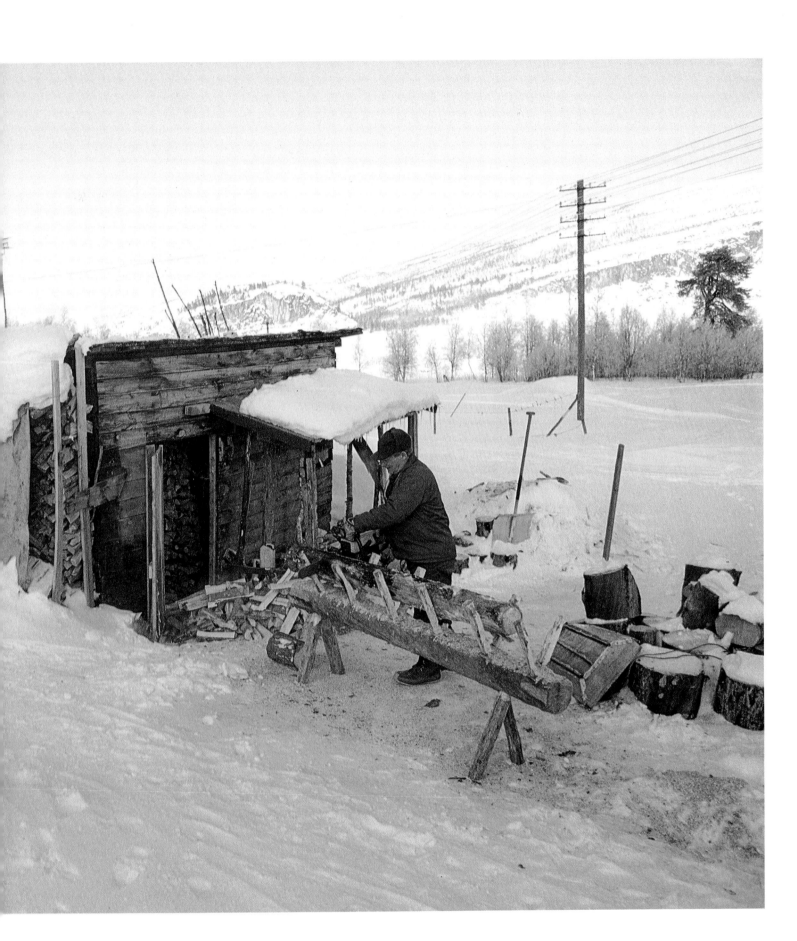

On the frozen waters of Lake Mälar, Sunday fishermen pursue the sport of ice-hole fishing, which once helped to keep their ancestors alive through the winter. Behind them, only a few hundred metres away, the tower of Stockholm Town Hall marks the heart of the Swedish capital.

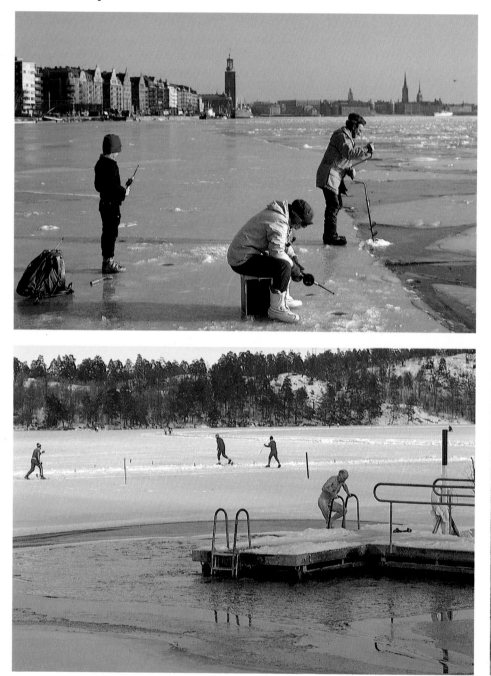

In Stockholm's Nacka reserve—one of several leisure areas in the city's environs—skiers pass by a hardy swimmer emerging from the icy waters of a lake. Few parts of the city are out of bounds to skiers, but this reserve has the advantage of marked trails and floodlit skiing facilities.

On Lake Mälar, competitors in an ice-sailing race trim their sails to catch the breeze. Ice-yachts can reach speeds four times the velocity of the wind, but the sport's participants often encounter difficulties in finding snow-free ice and favourable air conditions at the same time.

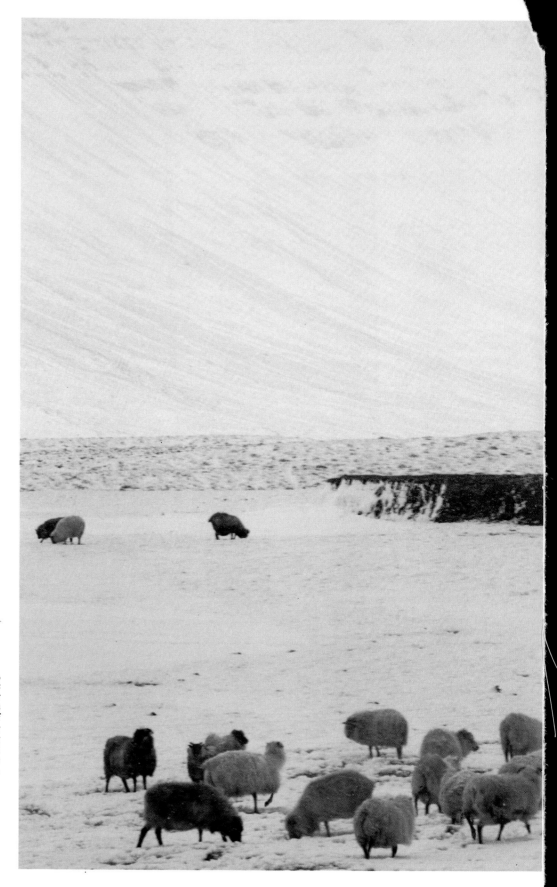

Roaming outside a storm shelter, sheep scratch through Icelandic snows for grazing to supplement their limited supplies of fodder. Iceland's sheep are too numerous for all of them to benefit from covered winter accommodation; selective breeding has improved the health and strength of the stock, making them more able to survive the rigours of winter.

A GENIUS FOR INVENTION

An international array of matchbox labels makes a colourful display at the Jönköping Match Museum, in southern Sweden. It was at Jönköping, in 1865, that the mechanized production of safety matches began. Sweden is the leading producer, with a daily output worldwide of some 50 million boxes.

A shack in the forest, a beggar's stave.
A life of poverty and a cross on the grave.

Thus a Finnish poet summed up the life of the landless peasantry in the 19th century. He was writing of his own people, but he might have been describing the plight of Scandinavians at large. At that time, little more than a century ago, the majority of the Nordic peoples were undernourished. Sweden's west coast region of Bohuslän was described as "one great poorhouse". In Swedish Norrland, and in the backwoods of interior and northern Finland, the diet when crops failed included a bread substitute made by pulverizing the inner bark of pine trees and baking it with dried mosses and chaff.

Nor was poverty confined to the predominantly rural population. In Oslo, within a stone's throw of the royal palace, large families were living in single rooms with neither running water nor sanitation. Stockholm and Copenhagen had relatively large slum districts, and on the outskirts of Helsinki many people lived in primitive wooden shacks that were piled tightly against each other. It was a time of grave social injustice; in Sweden and Finland, farm workers still put themselves up for auction at the annual autumn labour sales, and in some areas pauper children were actually sold outright. It was a time, too, of widespread sickness. Although smallpox—the greatest killer in 18th-century Europe—had been virtually conquered by the Jenner method of vaccination, tuberculosis was rife, helping to reduce life expectancy throughout Scandinavia to well under 50 years for both men and women.

"Emigrate or die" declared a Finnish newspaper headline of the 1870s. And hundreds of thousands of Scandinavians heeded such warnings by crossing the Atlantic in pursuit of a better life in America. Disastrous harvests from 1867 to 1869 caused an exodus of 80,000 from Sweden alone; so many followed that, by 1910, one Swede in five lived in America. In several years, Norwegian emigration figures approached 30,000, reducing the farming populations of certain areas by more than 50 per cent. When the first emigrant ship sailed from Stavanger in 1825, the population of Norway was over one million; yet within three generations it had sent three quarters of a million on the same transatlantic voyage.

In Denmark, as in Sweden and Norway, emigration reached a maximum in the 1880s. In Iceland and Finland, the greatest exodus came after the turn of the century. Iceland's population of little more than 70,000 sent out at least 12,000 to the United States and to Canada, where a "New Iceland" was established on the west shore of Lake Winnipeg. By 1910, a mass movement among the rural poor had contributed 20,000 Finns to the American population. In that same year, the U.S. had nearly three million inhabitants who

113

4

had been born in Scandinavia, or whose parents had been born there. Most of them sought a living from the prairie lands of the Mid-West, where they built their own cabins, often with earthen roof and walls, and only a single room to house a large family. For some, there was the discovery that they had exchanged one form of destitution for another—in America, as the Swedish author Wilhelm Moberg expressed it, "the dark is darker; the cold colder; the heat, hotter; and the mosquitoes a thousand times worse than in Sweden". But for most there was at least consolation in the belief that they had escaped a homeland which offered no hope for tomorrow.

They were wrong. In less than a century, Scandinavia had emerged from the economic backwoods and established itself as one of the richest regions in the world. Indeed, many Swedes, Finns, Norwegians and Danes might now argue that their home countries, not the United States, are the lands where dreams come true. As a measure of their wealth, a survey in the early 1980s showed that the national income per person in Norway was higher than in the United States, and that average earnings in Sweden, Denmark and Finland were higher than in France and Britain. In almost every area of private consumption—cars, TVs, telephones, refrigerators, washing machines—the Nordic countries were among the leading nations, and their share of national resources allocated to public services was the highest in the world.

How was this remarkable transformation achieved? Scandinavia was not in the forefront of the Industrial Revolution; indeed, in 1900, a majority of the population still lived by farming, forestry or fishing. Nevertheless, the great economic advance can be traced back to the belated arrival of industrialization after the middle of the 19th century. The European countries in which manufacturing was well established were hungry for Scandinavia's raw materials—Swedish iron ore for the furnaces of Britain and Germany, Swedish, Finnish and Norwegian timber for pit props, railway sleepers, telegraph poles and, above all, building construction. There was growing demand, too, for Danish dairy products and Norwegian fish to feed the urbanized masses of Britain and Germany. The trading boom stimulated the development of railways and the modernization and enlargement of merchant fleets. It also encouraged the import of new technology, which led to a dramatic expansion of the timber industry and—in Sweden especially—a thriving iron and steel industry.

Scandinavia laboured under a severe handicap: it had no suitable coal reserves at a time when industrial development was basically geared to the power of the coal-fired steam engine. Norway and Sweden, with their abundance of waterfalls, were able to develop an alternative source of energy: hydroelectricity. By 1900, they derived about two thirds of their electricity from waterfalls. But even this could not compensate for their poverty in the key mineral of the industrial revolution. Indeed, from the very beginning of industrialization, the Scandinavian countries were under pressure to seek more ways of utilizing the basic produce of their forests, farms, fisheries and mines. And this could only be done by introducing new technological processes and devising new products.

The result validated the cliché that necessity is the mother of invention. In seeking ways to extend their resources, the Scandinavians became responsible for an astonishing array of inventions, such as the safety match, the self-aligning ball bearing, the steam turbine, the continuous milk and cream separator, the exploding harpoon gun for whaling, the first adjustable spanner and the first primus stove. Herein lies the key to Scandinavia's remarkable rags-to-riches progress. Other countries have responded to industrial revolution with imagination and adaptability, but in doing so it is doubtful whether any nation of comparable size and limited resources has matched Scandinavia's record of innovation.

Among the Scandinavians, the Swedes, above all, have displayed a flair for inventiveness almost amounting to national genius. Sweden is currently taking out more patents than any other country with the exception of the United States, which has a population 28 times greater. And it is a measure of the skill with which the inventions have been developed and marketed that Sweden is now the industrial giant of the north. Fifteen of the top 20 industrial enterprises in Scandinavia are Swedish, and many of the largest industries in Sweden were based on Swedish inventions and innovations.

Unsurprisingly, Swedish inventiveness was at first concentrated on means of utilizing the country's two great assets: timber and iron ore. For example, G.F. Göransson, who founded a steel plant at Sandviken in 1862, was the first Scandinavian manufacturer to introduce Britain's new Bessemer steel-refining process for effective commercial exploitation. Later, around the turn of the century, a Swedish engineer, J.A. Brinell, developed a method for determining the hardness of steel, so the Swedes were able to take a lead in producing high-quality metal for drills.

Meanwhile, the demand for timber had greatly increased, following the discovery of commercially viable methods of making paper from wood pulp. Norway had pioneered the production of mechanical pulp in the 1860s, which advanced the birth of the modern newspaper. A Swedish chemist, Carl Ekman, subsequently improved the process by using sulphides to dissolve lignum from wood and leave pure cellulose. In 1872, the world's first chemical pulp factory was built at Bergvik in Sweden. Not until the 1890s was the industry developed on a significant scale, but then the growth was spectacular.

Between 1894 and 1914, Sweden increased production tenfold to establish itself as the world's leading exporter of mechanical and chemical pulp.

By that time Sweden had also become the leading manufacturer of safety matches. In 1844, the safety match was invented at the Royal Caroline Institute in Stockholm by Gustav Pasch, a chemist who replaced poisonous yellow phosphorus in the match head with non-toxic amorphous phosphorus. However, the full economic potential of this humble invention was not realized until after 1864, when Alexander Lagerman, a Swedish engineer, designed the first automated match machine.

In the 1920s, a single match company, Swedish Match, controlled three

quarters of the world's production of matches. It had been founded in 1917 under the presidency of Ivar Kreuger, the son of a match manufacturer and, according to the British economist John Maynard Keynes, the possessor of "maybe the greatest financial intelligence of his time". Kreuger's ambition was to bring all the match businesses of the world under his own control, and to achieve this aim he offered desperately needed financial services in return for monopolistic powers. In 1927, Kreuger organized a loan of $75 million to France, and the following year he arranged for Germany to receive a loan of $125 million. By then, Kreuger had gained control of some 250 match factories, with a total output of about 30

4

billion boxes of matches every year.

Despite his vast resources, Kreuger was not remotely as wealthy as he made himself out to be. By juggling his holdings, inventing fictitious enterprises, forging government bonds and inflating the value of his companies, he contrived to convince the world that he was worth $400 million when, in fact, the net assets of his companies were about $200 million, some $65 million less than his personal liabilities. Yet for 15 years Kreuger beguiled the world with his outrageous financial wizardry. He visited President Hoover in the White House and Mussolini in Rome, dated Greta Garbo, and kept mistresses in all the great capitals of Europe. Most remarkably, he managed to survive the great Wall Street crash of 1929.

Kreuger, Scandinavia's first world-famous industrial tycoon, liked to quote Napoleon's definition of happiness: "The ability to see difficulties gather at the same time that you can conquer them." But like Napoleon, he met his Waterloo. It came in March 1932, when he failed to negotiate loans needed to meet his multimillion dollar debts. Recognizing that financial disaster was imminent, he entertained his young Finnish mistress at his Paris apartment, and next day shot himself. In Sweden there was a day of national mourning. Flags were flown at half-mast. Politicians paid their tributes. And later, thousands lined the route of his funeral procession in Stockholm.

Soon afterwards, an official examination of the Kreuger empire revealed that he had "grossly misrepresented the true financial position". But it was to take five years of investigation into 400 companies before the true enormity of this misrepresentation could be

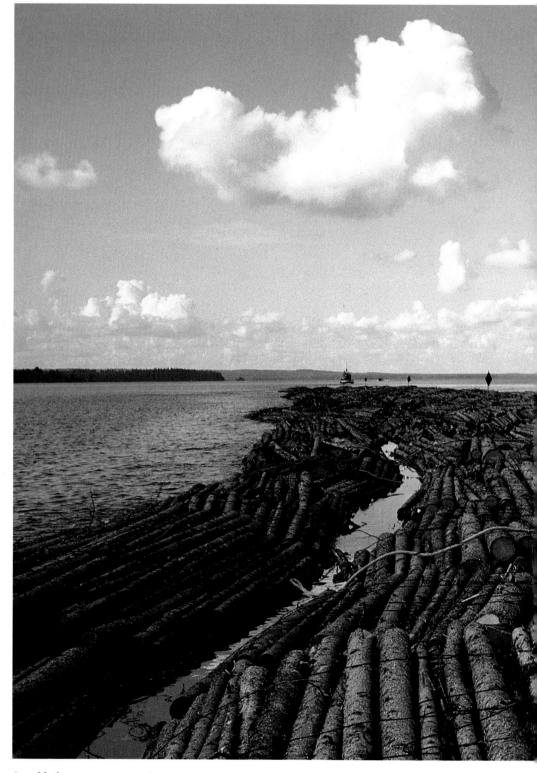

An athletic tug crewman vaults to check the bindings on a consignment of logs being towed from the forested centre of Finland to paper mills in the south. Wood is the mainstay of the Finnish economy; timber-based products make up about one third of the nation's exports.

4

appreciated. In the process, 20 directors and accountants were brought to trial and jailed. A newspaper headline proclaimed sadly: "The Collapse of Sweden's Second Empire". John Kenneth Galbraith, the American economist, subsequently described Kreuger as "by all odds, the biggest thief in the history of larceny". Yet, remarkably, it was not the end of Kreuger's Swedish Match. Though its debts exceeded $28 million, Swedish financiers recognized it as a basically sound business that could be salvaged. Sixteen years later, the company was at last able to pay dividends on its shares.

Today, Swedish Match is a solid and respectable group, still the largest producer of matches in the world. But the "little wooden soldiers", as Kreuger used to call his matches, only account for about a quarter of the company's business. The bulk of its profits are derived from an enormous variety of other wood and paper products. In this respect, the progress of Swedish Match is a typical Swedish success story—a company that started out by exploiting a single invention and then diversified.

Many of Sweden's other great international companies owe their existence to inventions made by Swedish engineers decades ago. They include ASEA, the huge electrical engineering and electronics group founded in 1883 to manufacture the dynamos invented by Jonas Wenström; the Ericsson group, a telecommunications giant whose founder patented the desk telephone, the first to combine mouthpiece and receiver in one unit; the Facit Group, a major office equipment and computer manufacturer that grew out of Willgodt Odhner's invention in 1874 of the world's first practical calculating machine; and SKF, founded in 1907 on

Sven Wingquist's invention of the self-aligning ball-bearing, and now the world's leading manufacturer of bearings, producing 25,000 variants, from the size of a pin head to giants weighing up to 3 tonnes.

In some cases, inventions dramatically transformed companies that were already established. A classic example was the Swedish firm of AGA, founded in 1904 for the production of dissolved acetylene gas. Gustaf Dalén joined the company as chief engineer and thereafter its future was inextricably linked to his inventions. One of his most novel ideas was the AGA sun valve, a solar-operated switch for turning lighthouse beacons on and off with the arrival of darkness or daylight. Despite derisive reaction from other scientists and from patents offices, his invention worked. Fifty years after it was marketed, there were more than 25,000 solar-operated AGA beacons lighting the sea lanes of the world—some of them having operated without repair for half a century.

By a tragic irony, the man who brought light into darkness was blinded when he was drenched in flaming acetylene during an experiment. His brother, a renowned eye surgeon, operated on him in vain. Yet, even without his sight, Dalén continued his innovative work for another quarter of a century. He carried out research into radio communications that was to pave the way for transistors, television sets and stereophonic sound systems; and it was during his years of blindness that he devised the fuel-efficient stove that has become synonymous with his company's name.

Another Swedish group whose products are sold worldwide is Alfa-Laval. The company was founded by Gustav de Laval, an engineer and chemist who

revolutionized dairy farming by his invention, in 1878, of a continuous centrifugal milk and cream separator. This simple invention, which almost every farmer could afford to buy, was especially valuable to agriculture-based Denmark. And as the company's production advanced, more and more applications were discovered for the invention, which could be used to purify, clarify and concentrate all manner of substances—foods, fuels, chemicals, pharmaceuticals.

In all, de Laval had 92 patents to his credit. They covered, among other things, a milking machine, the application of the rotation principle for the mass-production of glass bottles and, most importantly, the invention of the steam turbine in 1893. Yet he was by no means the most prolific Swedish inventor. He was eclipsed by a contemporary, Alfred Nobel, who held more than 350 Swedish and foreign patents. Paradoxically, Nobel, who developed new explosives and made a personal fortune from armaments, is now best known to the world as the philanthropic pacifist who, in his will, left 33 million kronur to be invested and the interest to be "annually distributed in the form of prizes to those who have conferred the greatest benefit on mankind".

Alfred Nobel was born in Stockholm in 1833, the son of an enterprising engineer-inventor who built steamships and submarine mines for tsarist Russia. In 1859, the family business went bankrupt and Alfred came to the rescue by patenting a detonator for use with nitroglycerine. The invention engendered the first of his fortunes at a time when the building of railways, roads and tunnels had made blasting a big business. Indirectly, it also led to the building of his reputation as a "mad

THE BEQUEST OF A DANISH BREWER

Internationally, the name of Carlsberg—Denmark's biggest brewing enterprise—is synonymous with lager, the product it exports to some 130 countries. Danes, however, know the firm as the sponsor of the Carlsberg Foundation, a philanthropic institution that devotes its profits—some $5 million in 1985—to furthering human knowledge and understanding.

The man responsible for initiating such magnanimity was founder J.C. Jacobsen. A fervent patriot, he set up the Carlsberg Foundation in 1876 to support scientific advancement. Thirty years later, his son Carl widened the scope of the policy to include the arts and humanities. Since then, the company has sent expeditions to the Arctic, financed research into cancer and the atom, restored national buildings, created the Glyptotek, Copenhagen's great art museum, and commissioned works of art.

Not the least of Jacobsen's bequests to the nation was his own sumptuous residence in the capital. According to his wishes, it serves as a "Mansion of Honour", to be occupied for life by a distinguished Dane. Its four residents to date have included the Nobel prize winner nuclear physicist, Neils Bohr.

Modern technology aids the traditional process of brewing in copper vats.

A Carlsberg dray passes the factory gates.

Crates of empty bottles lie ready for refilling at the company's plant in Copenhagen.

4

scientist" and a "merchant of death".

On September 3, 1864, the Nobel workshop at Heleneborg, on the outskirts of Stockholm, blew up, killing Alfred's younger brother, a mechanic, a boy assistant, a maid and a passing workman. Banished from the city, Nobel resumed production aboard a hired barge on Lake Mälar and later established an explosives factory in Hamburg. But then news came of another disaster. Off Aspinal, on the Atlantic coast of Panama, a steamer carrying a cargo of nitroglycerine blew up with the loss of 74 lives. Fourteen people died when another consignment shattered the San Francisco warehouse of Wells Fargo and Co. Across the world in Sydney, a warehouse and adjoining houses were razed. Then Nobel's own factory in Hamburg was destroyed.

Public alarm turned to panic, with some countries restricting the transport of nitroglycerine and some banning it altogether. Nobel set to work, seeking a way to minimize the dangers of handling the notoriously unstable liquid. His search ended in 1867 when he found that mixing nitroglycerine with a kind of fine clay produced a substance that could be dropped, shaken, heated and hammered without exploding. He called his invention "dynamite". Soon his discovery was in demand worldwide. It was used to blast out the Simplon Tunnel between Italy and Switzerland, and to excavate the Panama Canal; it thundered ahead of every railway construction gang from Sweden to Japan.

Nobel went on to build up a great armaments empire. Optimistically, in a letter to Baroness von Suttnow, a leading campaigner for world peace, he wrote: "My factories may make an end of war sooner than your congresses.

The day when two army corps can annihilate each other in seconds, all civilized nations, it is to be hoped, will recoil from war and discharge their troops." Perhaps it was just as well that he did not live to see the massive destruction wreaked by his weapons in World War I.

At the dawn of Scandinavia's industrial revolution, Norway, like Sweden, benefited greatly from the new processes for mineral and paper production. But, above all, Norway benefited from the development of hydroelectric power, popularly known as "white coal". The potential for such development was enormous in a country which has a very high precipitation (as much as 200 centimetres a year in some areas) and hundreds of towering waterfalls. Towards the realization of this potential, 11 hydroelectric plants were built between 1896 and 1900, and by the turn of the century, industry was using three times as much horsepower from electricity as from steam engines.

Norway, however, had even fewer industrial raw materials than Sweden, and so the problem was to find productive outlets for such an abundance of energy. Norwegian innovation came to the rescue by creating an entirely new industry: the manufacture of synthetic fertilizers. Two Norwegians, Professor Kristian Birkeland, an academic physicist, and Samuel Eyde, an industrial engineer, devised a means of using electrical energy to extract nitrogen from the atmosphere; and, in 1905, the commercial exploitation of their technique resulted in the foundation of Norsk Hydro, which became Norway's biggest industrial concern. Norsk Hydro is still Norway's largest company and still produces synthetic fertilizers,

though these are now based on petroleum rather than nitrogen. Surplus electrical power is used in the making of a large range of other products, from aluminium and magnesium to furniture and packaging materials.

As a result of its hydroelectric resources, Norway now produces more electricity per capita than any other country in the world. Its output is almost twice that of its nearest rivals, Canada and the United States. Largely on the strength of this resource, Norway has advanced from being one of Western Europe's poorest countries to one of its richest. In 1970, even before the profits from North Sea oil began to pour in, Norway was among the top 10 countries in the world with regard to gross national product on a per capita basis. Yet the nation could not have so rapidly capitalized on her "white coal" potential had it not been for the earnings generated by her traditional merchant marine and fishing enterprises.

In 1900, Norway's merchant fleet was the third largest in the world, and there were more Norwegians engaged in fishing and whaling than in industry. Here again, inventiveness played an important part. In 1864, for example, a Norwegian fisherman, Svend Foyn, revolutionized whaling by developing a gun to fire harpoons with explosive heads. The gun was so effective that he killed 32 blue whales on one expedition, whereas on a previous trip, using a conventional harpoon, he had caught only one whale. Thereafter, Norwegian whalers began to venture further afield, spending entire Antarctic summers in the waters around the South Pole icecap, where finback whales were to be found in large numbers.

Increased catches spurred other innovations. In 1905, the first floating factory whaler was launched from a Norwegian dock; and in 1924, a Norwegian whale gunner devised a special kind of slipway for hauling whales on to the deck of a factory ship, where they could be flensed and prepared for the boiler. Between 1927 and 1931, the total output of Antarctic whale oil more than quadrupled, with Norway taking two thirds of the world harvest.

In 1969, in the face of worldwide concern about declining whale populations, Norway retired most of its whaling fleet. In other respects, however, Norwegian fishing boats continue to gather a valuable harvest from the sea. In 1914, fishing provided 50,000 Norwegians with their main livelihood,

and some 90 per cent of Norway's fish catch was exported. Today there are still some 25,000 professional fishermen in Norway—far more than the combined totals of all the other Scandinavian countries—and 90 per cent of the catch (approximately 3 million tonnes a year) is sold abroad, making Norway the largest exporter of fish and fish products in Europe.

The extent of this surplus reflects both the richness of Norway's fishing grounds and the ingenuity of her fishermen. In the 1870s, the opening of a canning factory at Stavanger ushered in the age of the tinned sardine. Norway was one of the first countries to produce a professional class of fishermen oper-

ating decked, deep-sea boats equipped with cable-strengthened nets; also one of the first to introduce carrier vessels to transport freshly caught fish to the coastal processing plants, allowing the fleets to remain in continuous operation at sea. At the same time, Norway led the way with large-scale refrigeration (there are some 230 freezing plants along the Norwegian coast, and each year between 10 and 12 per cent of Norway's total catch is frozen).

Another major innovation since the early 1960s has been the establishment of fish farms, which are now operating in hundreds of sheltered bays, fjords and skerries bordering the Atlantic. By the mid-1980s, the bulk of Norway's

Sightseers stroll past a model of Amalienborg Palace, residence of the Danish royal family.

Hans Andersen assumes a new dimension.

In this replica of a Copenhagen harbour area, no building is more than a metre tall.

A WORLDWIDE BUSINESS BUILT ON TOY BRICKS

In 1932, Ole Kirk Christiansen, a carpenter from the Jutland village of Billund, started making wooden toys to supplement his income. The firm he founded—Lego, from the Danish *leg godt*, meaning "play well"—became a gold mine some 25 years later, when his son introduced a new line: interlocking toy bricks that could be shaped into almost any form a child's imagination could devise. The response was immediate, and Lego became a multimillion dollar enterprise, with outlets in over 50,000 shops worldwide.

The most spectacular display of Lego's achievements can be seen in Billund itself. There, on a 10-hectare site, the company has created the miniature world of Legoland Park. Made up of more than 30 million bricks forming models that range from replicas of spacecraft to Copenhagen landmarks, the park has become Denmark's biggest tourist attraction outside the capital.

Legoland provides its own version of the famous bronze statue of the Little Mermaid.

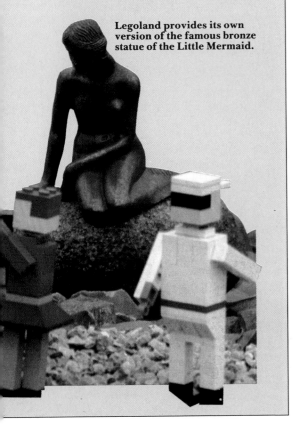

salmon and trout—about 22,300 tonnes a year—came from private, net-enclosed reserves, where the fish are scientifically spawned and fed on a diet provided by the ocean. In these protected conditions, salmon reach an average weight of 4 kilograms after two years. Immediately after harvesting, a large proportion of the crop is exported by air, in specially designed refrigerated containers, to more than 20 countries, including the U.S. and Japan.

Norway's other traditional maritime strength is its merchant navy—until 1976, the fourth largest in the world with a gross registered tonnage of 26.8 million. Until the late 1970s, Norway's 200 shipping companies prospered by operating purpose-built cargo vessels and oil tankers. The majority of these ships were designed for specific tasks and manned by specialized crews; and they were the most up-to-date in the world because they were replaced by new models on average every six years, compared with a world average of 11 years. However, one feature of Norway's specialization almost proved to be her undoing. In 1973, when the energy crisis broke on an unsuspecting world, 20 million tonnes of Norwegian shipping was in oil tankers, including 72 tankers of over 100,000 tonnes—far too many for the reduced amount of oil available. Many of the tankers had to be laid up. A hundred vessels were idle in 1976, and though the stock of laid-up ships decreased to 44 in 1978, the continuing recession and competition from other shipbuilding nations saw the Norwegian merchant navy steadily fall to seventh position in the world.

It was therefore ironic that oil and natural gas should also prove Norway's greatest economic blessing. The first discoveries in the Norwegian sector of the North Sea were made in 1969 and 1970. No one knows with certainty the amount of oil and gas that exists in the Norwegian fields, but estimates indicate total reserves of 4,000 to 5,000 million tonnes. By the mid-1980s, production had risen to more than 50 million tonnes a year. Since Norway's own annual demand is less than 9 million tonnes, the country has a huge surplus for export—the equivalent of the combined requirements of Sweden and Denmark. The income earned from this oil bonanza has raised Norway from ninth position in the world league of wealthy nations in the early 1970s to her current situation, vying with Switzerland for the highest standard of living in the world.

In the late 19th century, when neighbouring Sweden and Norway were in the throes of economic change, Iceland was still locked into a pre-industrial structure as primitive as it was poor. In 1900 there was not a single factory in the country, scarcely a passable road, no bridges, no man-made harbour and few stone-built houses. The people remained dependent on the resources of the sea and animal husbandry.

The first sign of progress in Iceland was the adaptation of the fishing fleet from open rowing boats to decked vessels that were capable of venturing to more distant waters. The founding of a national bank and the progress of the co-operative movement, which was established in 1882, also promised the Icelanders better trading opportunities. In the 20th century, the size of their catches—mainly herring, cod and haddock—steadily mounted as a result of more sophisticated techniques, the introduction of super-efficient, large-decked stern-trawlers, and the development of fishing as a year-round activity instead of a seasonal one.

Eventually, fishing was so critical to its economy that Iceland unilaterally extended its fishing limits—from 6 to 19 kilometres in 1958, then to 80 kilometres in 1971, and 322 kilometres in 1975. These actions led to the so-called "Cod Wars"—*opéra bouffe* affairs which consisted of a series of minor skirmishes between Icelandic coastguard cutters and British trawlers and frigates. In 1974, the Hague Court ruled against Iceland, but world opinion and political considerations persuaded Britain to concede to its tiny NATO ally.

Victory in this matter, however, did not bring the expected gains. Cod stocks continued to diminish, possibly because of climatic changes or perhaps due to new patterns in the movement of fish. Whatever the cause, Iceland was compelled to develop its economy in other directions—to such effect that manufacturing and services now claim a majority of the employed population. Industries, mostly small in scale, range from dairying and meat production to greenhouse cultivation and knitwear. But there are few large-scale enterprises, mainly because the domestic market is too small to support major industries, and the international market too distant to allow economic trading.

Yet Iceland does have enormous potential wealth in its abundance of hydroelectric resources and geothermal energy from its hot springs. As an Icelandic Minister of Industry stressed not long ago: "Our oil is flowing all over the country—in our rivers, in our waterfalls, and under the ground." This "oil" cannot be put in barrels and shipped overseas. However, it has been suggested that the process might work in reverse: by encouraging foreign companies to bring their plants to the energy source. In theory, this might be achieved. In practice, it is unlikely, because of the small size of the domestic market and the high transport costs from such an isolated island. Until this problem can be solved, Iceland's economy must remain largely dependent on the products of its farms and fisheries.

Finland, like Iceland, lagged behind the rest of Scandinavia in progressing towards industrialization until after World War II. To a degree, the Finns were held back by lack of capital investment in the late 19th century and then by the struggle for independence from Russia. More generally, however, their slow development was due to the nature of their land (roughly 80 per cent forest and water), together with their harsh climate and remote location. In 1917, when Finland became an independent republic, some 70 per cent of the population was still employed in agriculture and forestry; and for most Finns the new technology of the industrial age simply meant more varied and more economical means of processing forest and farm products.

When the country eventually began to industrialize on a broad front, it changed from an agrarian to an urban society at an astonishing rate. In 1950, half of the gainfully employed population derived a living from the land; by the mid-1980s, about one tenth did. In common with all the Scandinavian states, Finland now has an economy in which service activities and commerce dominate the employment structure. Metallurgical and engineering operations employ a larger percentage of the work force than forest-based industries; and the widely known exports of textiles, clothing, skiing equipment (Finland is the world's largest manufacturer) and domestic wares are of modest consequence beside the less well-known exports of major capital goods.

Finland has competed successfully in Latin America, Africa, the Middle East and South-East Asia for the sale of entire paper-making, metallurgical and hydroelectric power plants. Unlike the other Scandinavian nations, it has also developed a major market in the Soviet Union. For a generation, the Soviets have been purchasing Finnish-made icebreakers and lake and river craft, including large-scale floating dormitories for construction workers. The largest single enterprise conducted across Finland's eastern border has been the construction of a large iron and steel complex at Kostamus in the Karelian Soviet Republic. When this was under way in the 1970s, it provided as many jobs for commuting Finnish workers as the entire North Sea oil industry had done for Norwegians.

These achievements have been accomplished despite the fact that Finland has limited resources and has to import nearly two thirds of its energy needs. They seem even more impressive given that Finland's 1941 to 1944 war with the Soviet Union cost her massive reparations and 10 per cent of her territory, including a part of Lapland rich in nickel deposits. Those reparations, payable over eight years, took the form of ships, locomotives, machinery, electrical equipment, building components and even complete industrial plants. At that time, Finland had only a few, modest-sized heavy engineering and metal industries, and limited numbers of trained engineers and skilled technicians.

Ironically, these enforced repayments were to prove just the economic

An icebreaker ploughing through the frozen waters of the Baltic testifies to the engineering skill of Finland's shipbuilders. Pioneering Arctic technology, one leading firm is currently designing a new model driven by nuclear power.

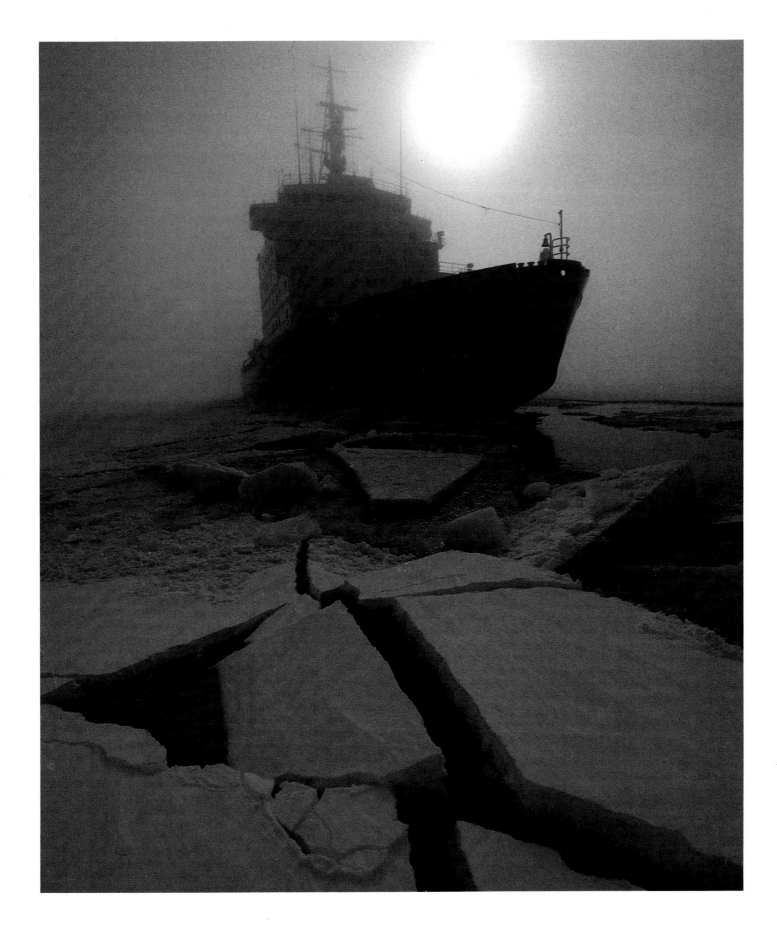

4

stimulus that Finland needed. They compelled the nation to develop a broader industrial base on which to build for the future. As Finnish observers noted at the time, that base had rested too long on a single wooden leg; now they were gaining a second leg of metal. It soon emerged that there were other possibilities for the new industries to exploit. Geological exploration revealed that Finland's mineral resources, though limited, were reasonably varied and could be mined: pyrites, iron ore, zinc and various other minerals in modest quantities. In the early 1970s, the products of the metal and engineering industries accounted for more than 25 per cent of Finnish export, and Finland had become one of the world's largest producers of vanadium, used in steel manufacture.

Like Germany after World War II, Finland also profited in the long run from being compelled to build industries entirely anew without the burden of antiquated machinery and methods. For example, the nation had to cede its entire fleet of icebreakers as part of the reparations programme. In the course of replacing these vital components of the merchant marine, Finnish engineers developed an unrivalled expertise in icebreaker construction, pioneering the use of propellers at both ends of the ships, twin rudders, and hulls designed to withstand pressures many times greater than conventional designs.

As a result, the country emerged as a world leader in icebreaker technology. By the mid-1980s, the Wärtsila shipyards of Helsinki and Turku had built 60 per cent of all icebreakers constructed since World War II, and had captured 30 per cent of the world's cruise ship market. Wärtsila also led in Arctic offshore technology, and its research equipment now includes the world's largest laboratory for the testing of model ships designed to sail in frozen waters. In this laboratory, a 70-metre-long basin can be frozen over to simulate all kinds of ice conditions, with video cameras recording the interaction of ice and propellers, rudders and hulls. Wärtsila's experience and experimental facilities have been called upon by other countries—especially, Canada, the United States and the U.S.S.R.—which are concerned with trafficking in frozen waters. Their technologies are likely to be of considerable significance for the commercial exploitation of oil fields hidden under the polar ice.

Despite these diverse industrial developments, Finland's great forests remain the backbone of the economy. New technologies have transformed the physical management of the forests and, at the same time, dramatically expanded the range of products to be derived from timber. Until the late 19th century, the logger with an axe exploited timber almost as a wild crop. Since the 1950s—by which time Finland's forested area had been surveyed in detail and brought within the zone of commercial exploitation—timber has been treated as a rotation crop, felled by motor saw, and carefully nurtured by seed-breeding, draining, planting, fertilizing and selective harvesting. As a result, the consumption of timber by industry has doubled within a generation without depleting the forest.

An ever-increasing number of mechanical processes has diversified the output of forest products, ranging from deal board and plywood to wallboard and laminates, from pre-fabricated houses and saunas to hundreds of different kinds of paper and, not least, to the dozens of chemicals produced as by-products through fermentation and distillation. In the mid-1980s, Finnish pulp and paper goods made up more than 60 per cent of its forest products, and the vast bulk was exported, satisfying nearly one quarter of Europe's demand. *The Times* and the *Daily Mail* of London and *Le Monde* and *Le Figaro* of Paris are among the many foreign publications printed on Finnish paper. Forest industries continue to account for about one third of export earnings, and are more important to Finland than any other Scandinavian country.

Although Finland and Iceland were so late to industrialize, they did at least have some advantage in their possession of vast resources of, respectively, timber and geothermal power. Denmark, in contrast, was unique among Scandinavian countries in lacking large forests and being virtually devoid of metals, coal and other energy sources. Thus, while Sweden and Norway were engaged in industrial transformation, Denmark's attention was focused on agriculture, which had to be modernized and greatly expanded if the country was to export on a scale sufficient to balance her import needs.

This was a daunting challenge for two reasons. First, Denmark had lost two fifths of her territory—much of it good farmland—in the 1864 war with Germany. Secondly, her traditional grain crops could no longer compete with the cheap American imports that flooded into Western Europe after prairie railways had opened up trade routes to the Atlantic ports.

Denmark's loss of farmland was offset partly by the activities of a young road engineer, Enrico Dalgas, who, in 1866, inspired the foundation of the Danish Heath Society to promote land reclamation, particularly in Jutland. By carefully tilling the sandy soils, draining the peat bogs, introducing root crops to rotation farming and planting coniferous shelter belts, the Danes brought hitherto unproductive areas into cultivation. By 1914, the addition to the cultivated area in Jutland alone had compensated for what had been lost to Germany. Meanwhile, the problem of American grain imports was overcome by a dramatic switch from arable to animal products.

The move began in the 1870s. Within little more than a decade, animal husbandry had reached such a scale that Danish farmers were exporting to Britain's industrial cities substantial quantities of dairy produce and bacon, shipped by way of the newly created North Sea port of Esbjerg. By the end of the 19th century, Denmark was the world's largest exporter of these products. Critical to this achievement was the development of co-operative processing and marketing organizations, which ensured that the products were of standard types and qualities carefully adapted to the demands of different markets. The first co-operative dairy was founded by the farmers of West Jutland in 1882; in less than a decade, there were 700, and, by the turn of the century, more than a thousand.

Farmers are notoriously conservative, and it is unlikely that the rise of rural co-operatives would have been so quick and effective if the way had not been prepared through a unique educational scheme, initiated in the 1840s by Bishop N.F.S. Grundtvig. A patriotic idealist, Grundtvig was determined to improve educational standards among the rising generation of country folk. He achieved this by founding residential establishments, known as folk high

schools, for young adult members of the farming community. It was a measure of his achievement that by 1900 some 15 per cent of the students at folk high schools were from families of smallholders, and his educational scheme had been adopted by other Scandinavian countries. Meanwhile, the co-operative movement had taken hold in Norway, Sweden and Iceland, and it was spreading further: shortly before World War I, Finland was to be dubbed "a nation of co-operators" by the Swedish economist Thorsten Odhe. In more recent years, even the Lapps have followed Denmark's lead by establishing a co-operative factory for processing reindeer products.

As Scandinavia's most cultivable country, Denmark remained a predominantly agricultural land well into the 20th century. As late as the 1950s, farming products accounted for more than 50 per cent of Danish exports. However, the Danes used the healthy profits generated by their food exports to develop both light and heavy industries. In the latter half of the 19th

century, a Danish entrepreneur, T.F. Tietgen, founded a telegraph company and a shipping company. He also expanded the engineering firm of Burmeister and Wain, which, in 1912, built the first diesel-engined ship. Burmeister and Wain is now the world's biggest manufacturer of diesel engines.

It was hardly an industrial advance to match that of neighbouring Sweden. But then, after World War II, an injection of much needed capital investment via the United States' Marshall Aid programme launched Denmark into a second industrial revolution. By the mid-1950s, manufacturing capacity equalled that of agriculture; and today industry accounts for some 70 per cent of Denmark's exports, compared to agriculture's 30 per cent. With fewer workers and increasing mechanization and rationalization, the productivity of farms has increased to such a degree that one farm worker now produces enough food for 100 people, compared with 35 in 1950; and about two thirds of agricultural production can be exported. Related to this achievement has

4

been the production of agricultural equipment and machinery—small harvesters, tractors and machines—scaled down to suit the size of Denmark's myriad smallholdings and the size of the farmer's pocket.

Undoubtedly, the strongest commercial resource possessed by the Danes is their native wit and intelligence. These qualities have enabled them to work their own kind of economic miracle. They are almost entirely beholden to overseas suppliers for their raw materials, and yet a veritable flood of products has poured into the export market from Danish factories, workshops and shipyards—everything from fibreglass sailing dinghies to 500,000-tonne supertankers; from nail varnish to special cements for use in extreme climatic conditions; from pharmaceuticals (Denmark is the world's major manufacturer of insulin) to resuscitation equipment; from plastic balls designed for raising sunken ships to automatically operated bridges and desalination plants; from silverware and porcelain to every conceivable item for furnishing the home and clothing the body.

Danish electronic equipment has been landed on the moon. Many countries use its X-ray equipment to test seam welds on aircraft hulls. Danish building systems are bought by nations that wish to relieve housing shortages quickly and efficiently. Through experience in linking together the islands of their fragmented country, Danish engineers have established an international reputation for bridge-building and harbour construction. And parents all over the world who want to amuse and educate their children at the same time give them Lego bricks, ingeniously devised during the fifties by the son of a

MASTERWORKS OF SCANDINAVIAN DESIGN

From the 1930s through to the 1950s and 1960s, the bold modernity of Scandinavian-made ceramics, glassware, fabrics and furniture was to transform the look of home and office furnishings around the world. The hallmarks of visual grace, simplicity and craftsmanship that characterized Scandinavian design had their roots in a long tradition of Viking and folk art. A more immediate inspiration, however, was the concept of functional design formulated in the 1920s by the German Bauhaus school of artist-craftsmen, and reflected by Nordic designers who were aware of the need to bring beauty and style to mass-produced goods. The key elements of functionalism—simple construction techniques, clean lines and natural materials—were applied to almost every conceivable type of artifact, but showed to especially good effect in the design of seating. Without sacrificing comfort, the chair was stripped of upholstery and ornamentation in the now-classic plywood and laminated bentwood model *(below, right)* produced by the Finnish architect Alvar Aalto for the Paimio sanatorium in 1930. Six years later, he demonstrated the same practical approach in devising easily stacked stools for libraries *(below, left)*.

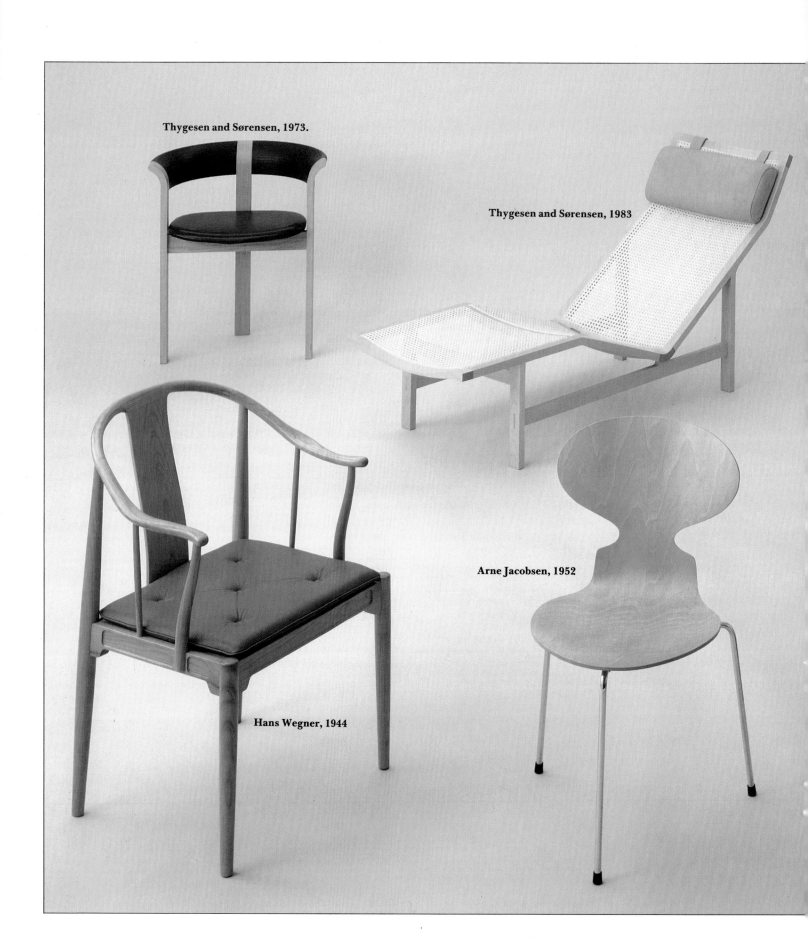

Thygesen and Sørensen, 1973.

Thygesen and Sørensen, 1983

Arne Jacobsen, 1952

Hans Wegner, 1944

130

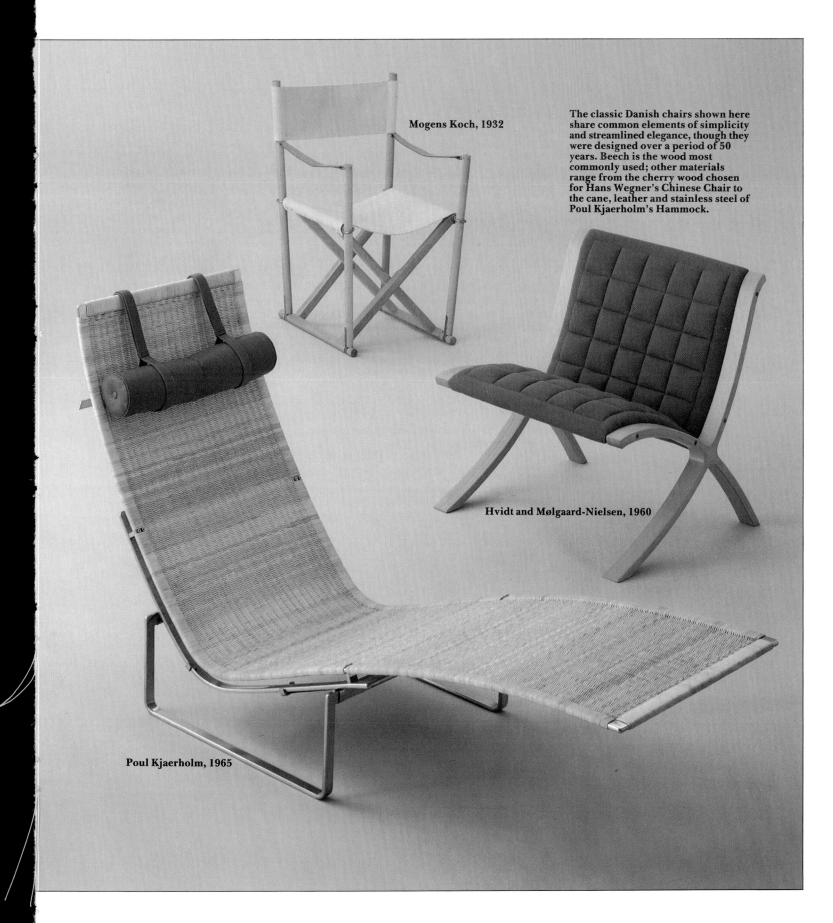

Mogens Koch, 1932

The classic Danish chairs shown here share common elements of simplicity and streamlined elegance, though they were designed over a period of 50 years. Beech is the wood most commonly used; other materials range from the cherry wood chosen for Hans Wegner's Chinese Chair to the cane, leather and stainless steel of Poul Kjaerholm's Hammock.

Hvidt and Mølgaard-Nielsen, 1960

Poul Kjaerholm, 1965

4

Jutland carpenter and now a multimillion dollar business.

The success story of Denmark's manufacturing industries reflects an attitude shared by Scandinavia as a whole. The Nordic countries recognized that, with limited raw materials and high labour costs, they would have difficulty in producing competitively priced goods for export. Independently, they arrived at the conclusion that if they could not compete on basic price, they must offer superior value for money. One way was to build a reputation for goods of durability and reliability—those qualities embodied in the utilitarian solid fuel stove which Gustaf Dalén had made virtually indestructible and so efficient that it could be kept burning for up to 24 hours without refuelling.

Dalén's cooker, still widely used in Western Europe, is obviously the work of a practical engineer, not a styling department. The same can be said of Sweden's Volvo and Saab vehicles. Volvos have the enviable reputation of being the world's most durable mass-produced cars, with a life expectancy of more than 20 years. Saabs, too, have a reputation for reliability enhanced by a successful record in motor rallies. Moreover, both cars are technically innovative. Volvo has pioneered many of the safety features now built into competitors' vehicles, and Saab were the first to market a turbo-powered saloon that increased performance without affecting economy.

Another factor in Scandinavia's commercial success has been design. Ever since the 1920s and the German-inspired movement for "beautiful things for everyday use", Scandinavian manufacturers have been associated with clean, smooth lines in furniture,

colourful and manageable kitchenware, and unfussy ornaments. In that decade, the need for things stylish but simple was advocated by Poul Henningsen, a Danish architect, designer and creator of ingenious lampshades. "Throw away your artists' berets and bow ties and get into overalls," he exhorted his colleagues. "Down with artistic pretentiousness. Simply make things that are fit for use: that is enough to keep you busy, and you will sell vast quantities and make lots of money."

It so happened that Scandinavian designers were in a better position than their foreign rivals to heed such advice. A native craft tradition had been kept alive through the 19th century by various national societies, including the Swedish Society of Industrial Design, founded in 1845. This was the first of its kind in the world, and was followed 30 years later by the Finnish Society of Crafts and Design. Furthermore, the late arrival of the industrial revolution in Scandinavia meant that many small folk craft enterprises flourished alongside mass-production factories well into the 20th century, so providing a source of inspiration to designers when public taste began to rebel against the domestic goods on offer.

The Danes and the Finns led the way. Their influence was most evident in the works of the Finnish architect Alvar Aalto and his Danish contemporary Arne Jacobsen, who was instrumental in popularizing the elegant light furnishings which, by the late 1930s, were to be seen in many Scandinavian homes. After World War II, the Danes in particular gave a distinctive and attractive look to the products of high technology as much as to the traditional craft industries. Emphasis on original design led to a profitable

expansion of Danish silver and porcelain, and before long a reputation for original styling had been won for Norwegian enamelling, Swedish glass, Finnish furniture and Icelandic woollens. By then, "Scandinavian Design" had become a recognizable and uniform quality, because the Nordic countries had developed their creative styles on similar lines and there had been considerable cross-fertilization.

The designers themselves brought the Scandinavian touch to overseas countries. The Finnish architect Eliel Saarinen led the way by influencing the development of the American skyscraper; his son Eero was the architect of the U.S. Embassy in London. Another Finnish architect, Wiljo Rewell, gave Toronto its City Hall. Alvar Aalto was responsible for distinctive buildings in the U.S., Germany, Italy and many other European countries. Arne Jacobsen designed St. Catherine's College, Oxford, and left his mark on such faraway places as Hawaii, Peru and Zambia, where his furniture was used in churches, hospitals, hotels, offices, town halls and universities. And in the 1950s, a young Danish architect, Joern Utzon, won an international design competition for the Sydney Opera House, an architectural masterpiece ultimately costing $104 million.

For all its originality and practicality, Scandinavian design has now probably passed the zenith of its influence. There is a saturation point in most styles, and, as European homes and European tastes grow increasingly standardized, the scope for variety, particularly in the simple Scandinavian style, diminishes all the time. In fact, the emphasis in the design field has now moved away from domestic products towards the area of high technology—advanced instruments, electronics, robotics, telecommunications, chemicals and pharmaceuticals.

Today, Scandinavian industry has entered a new era of international trade in which multinational companies such as Ericsson, ASEA and Electrolux are extending their bases overseas, by buying up existing companies or selling to markets as far away as Japan, Brazil or India. At the same time, there is more emphasis on marketing the accumulated expertise of high technology industries—for example, the know-how to build and operate softwood processing plants, hydroelectric power stations and cement-manufacturing plants. A senior executive of Alfa-Laval explains, "We have shifted from selling components to selling entire systems and the knowledge of how to make the best use of those systems." Such ambitious international marketing—practised to a greater or lesser degree by Sweden, Denmark, Finland and Norway—is certainly a far cry from the years, less than a century ago, when Scandinavia's largest contribution to the world was its poor and its dispossessed.

Lecturing to students in Helsinki in 1867, Zachris Topelius summed up the three keys to history: geographical position, natural conditions and the ability of people to use them. With its northerly location and limited resources, Scandinavia was certainly not favoured in the first two respects. But the challenge its hardships and handicaps presented greatly spurred ingenuity, enterprise and industry. It has been the ability of the Nordic peoples to explore and exploit the unpromising hand dealt by nature that has made a demi-paradise—in terms of material comfort and security—out of land that was once largely a forbidding wilderness.

A pair of sculpted figures serve as lamp standards above the main entrance of Helsinki railway station. Built by the Finnish architect, Eliel Saarinen, and completed in 1914, the station was an early illustration of the Scandinavian flair for combining the functional with the ornamental.

AN IMAGINATIVE CONCERN FOR YOUNG CHILDREN

A plaster troll (*left*)—the shaggy giant of Scandinavian legend—towers over children playing on slides in an amusement park near the Norwegian town of Lillehammer. Elsewhere in the park (*above*), a boy lies almost submerged in a tank of plastic balls as he prepares to toss one at a friend.

Few nations are as well provided with leisure facilities for their children as the Scandinavian lands. Spaces furnished with play equipment, usually made of plastic or wood and designed to be both safe and handsome, can be found in almost all town centres; and many shopping precincts, large department stores and even ferries also boast recreation areas. Public libraries have juvenile sections that often lend not just books but also toys, games and records. Such facilities for fun reflect the emphasis that Scandinavian governments have placed on child welfare in modern times.

There are pressing social reasons for their concern. Since World War II, it has become increasingly common for wives as well as husbands to go out to work. The result has been a rapid growth in the need for comprehensive services for the care of children under seven—the age when formal schooling begins in all Nordic countries. The Finns have responded by establishing more than 1,700 state-subsidized day-care centres. There are also playgroups run by local authorities, the church and other organizations, and playgrounds where children can be left under the supervision of "park nannies". These facilities are supplemented by state-approved child-minders, who can take up to four children into their own homes for the day.

Demand for child-care facilities continues to outrun supply throughout Scandinavia, however. In Sweden, for example, where some 80 per cent of mothers with children under seven are now working part or full-time, there was room in 1985 to accommodate only a third of the children in the available state-run, day-care nurseries.

A park nanny watches over young children left to play in a Helsinki sand-pit. Such private child-minders are often hired by working parents of pre-school-age infants; but Finland also has some 1,600 outdoor playgrounds supervised by state employees, mainly catering for rather older age groups.

At lunch in a Helsinki kindergarten, five and six-year-olds patiently look on while two boys choose from a plate of open sandwiches offered by a teacher. Some 290,000 Finnish children—over half of those under school age—attend some kind of day-care institution.

In the reading room of Stockholm's multi-purpose House of Culture, youngsters listen raptly to children's records through headphones. The six-storey complex was completed in 1974 and now attracts some 2.5 million visitors every year.

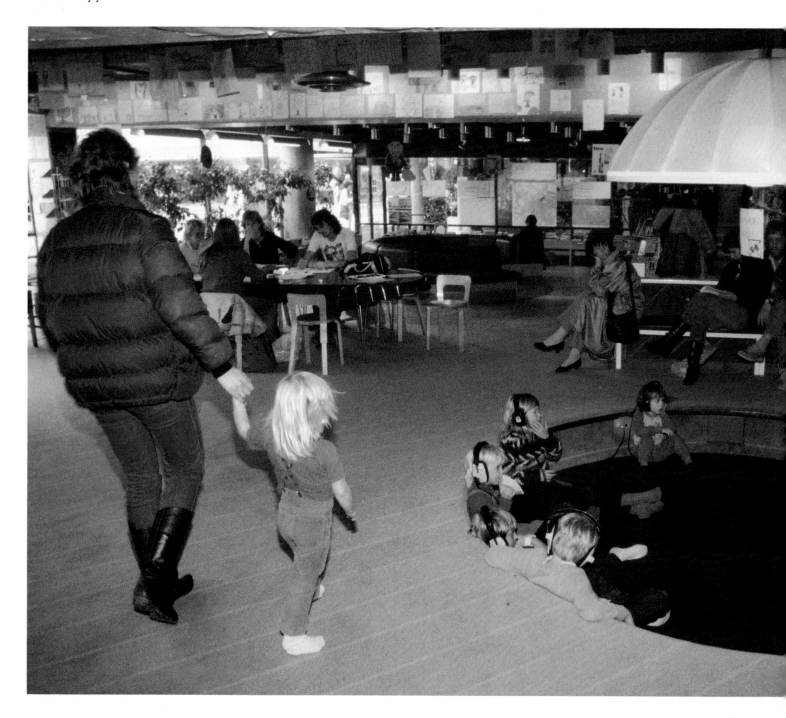

Imaginatively designed play areas are
a feature of many urban centres in
Scandinavia. Tapiola in Finland *(below)*
provides brightly coloured horses and
a slide to entertain young children,
while the Norwegian port of Bergen
(bottom) recalls its seafaring traditions
with a model boat.

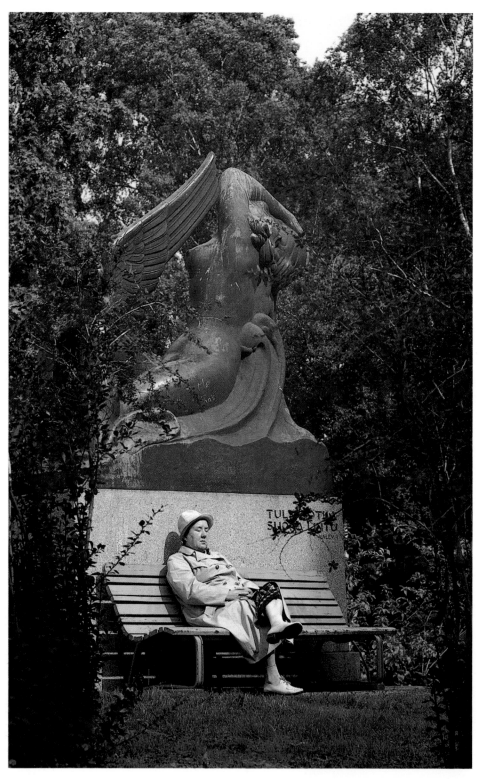

In a tranquil corner of Helsinki's Sibelius Park, a woman basks in the summer sun beneath a statue by the Finnish sculptor Aarre Aaltonen. The work represents an episode from Finland's national epic, the *Kalevala*.

THE QUEST FOR UTOPIA

In 1984, Scandinavia received an extraordinary compliment. An American university professor published the results of a nine-year investigation into the social progress made by 107 countries with populations of at least one million. Denmark achieved first place in his world order of merit. Norway came second. Sweden was in fifth place, behind Austria and the Netherlands. Finland shared 10th place with West Germany. By way of contrast, France was 16th, Britain 25th, the United States 42nd, the Soviet Union 44th and Ethiopia last.

Richard Estes of the University of Pennsylvania School of Social Work based his statistical analysis on an index of 44 different plus or minus factors, including literacy, health, welfare programmes, political stability, natural disasters, cultural diversity and women's status. Only four of the factors were economic indicators. The study, he stressed, was not addressing the highly subjective question of personal happiness and satisfaction with life. But it was designed to establish the general—rather than just the material—well-being of different nations.

Such an analysis inevitably invites controversy. Not even all Scandinavians were entirely satisfied with the findings; Estes received letters from Swedes who could not comprehend how Denmark had achieved a higher rating than their own country. Yet even with all allowances made, the Scandinavians' performance was remarkable. Indeed, the Nordic countries would have achieved five places in the top 10 if Iceland had not been disqualified by virtue of its small population. Certainly the island would have rated highly in terms of health. The average life expectancy for Icelanders—73.9 years for men and 79.4 for women—is the second highest in the world after Japan, closely followed by that of the Swedes and the Norwegians.

Could it be, then, that Scandinavia is leading the rest of the world in the quest for the ideal society? Sociologists have been pondering that question for half a century—ever since 1936, when Sweden's social progress was held up for the world to see in Marquis Childs' renowned book, *Sweden: The Middle Way*. The Swedes, this American journalist claimed, had discovered a happy mean between the extremes of laissez-faire capitalism and totalitarian communism. They were solving their problems in a sensible, pragmatic way at a time when other Western democracies appeared to be floundering and war clouds were gathering menacingly over central Europe. "The struggle between the regressive forces of an outworn individualism and the new collective order has been overwhelming," Childs wrote. "If anywhere in modern life a balance has been struck, it seems to me to have been in the Scandinavian peninsula, and particularly in Sweden."

Childs was not suggesting that he had discovered Utopia "or even an approximation of Utopia"; and the Scandinavians themselves did not claim to have created some kind of paradise on earth. Nevertheless, the Nordic experiment continues to be a fashionable subject for both foreign journalists and sociologists to study and analyse. To what extent the Scandinavian approach to social problems has succeeded remains debatable. But two facts are beyond dispute: no other countries have been so adventurous and altruistic in introducing new social measures, and no others have acted for so long as a kind of social laboratory, producing innovations which other countries have sometimes greeted with incredulity, then found themselves imitating.

A popular tale from ancient Scandinavian history recounts how a scouting party once travelled up the Seine at the head of a small Viking fleet. As the vessel approached a bend in the river beyond Rouen, a messenger from the Frankish overlord was sent out to discover the identity of the commander of the Viking fleet. Hailing the ship, the messenger shouted: "What is the name of your captain?" Back came the reply: "There is no captain here. On this ship all are equals."

The story, though surely apocryphal, does have some basis in fact. The Vikings held foreigners in slavery and acquired a reputation for appalling savagery in lands they invaded. But among themselves they achieved a relatively advanced social order and a greater degree of equality than other peoples of their time. Viking men could have freehold rights to land without paying dues or levies to an overlord. Women could own land and manage property (a bunch of keys hanging from the waist symbolized their authority)

5

and divorce could be obtained easily and without shame.

One thousand years later, their descendants, using the mechanisms of modern bureaucratic states, set out to fulfil the Nordic yearning for equality by redistributing income through taxation and social benefits. In 1891–92, Denmark became the first European country to introduce health insurance laws and old-age pensions on a contributory basis. This measure marked the beginning in Scandinavia of the most extensive social security systems in the world—systems now providing free health care and free education for all, paternity as well as maternity benefits, family allowances, pensions that are automatically adjusted to the cost of living, subsidized aids for the handicapped, sheltered homes for the aged, home helps for families in need, refuges for battered wives, nurseries for the children of working parents.

Today's Vikings, however, have gone far beyond basic welfare legislation in striving to create a more well-ordered, egalitarian society. They have sought to eliminate geographical inequalities by providing services and communications, at enormous cost, to the many small communities isolated on islands, in mountain villages and in the far north. They have introduced the "social wage"—a minimum income guaranteed by the state. (If a citizen earns less than this sum, the balance is made up by the local authorities.) They have been responsible for pioneering such innovations as anti-smoking campaigns, the compulsory wearing of seat belts in cars, and compulsory sex education in schools.

They have led the way, too, in their approach to crime and punishment. Finland, for example, has not em-

ployed the death penalty for more than 150 years. In 1933, Denmark abolished corporal punishment as well as capital punishment. Later, radical penal reforms in Sweden included granting some prisoners the right to work at wages related to those paid on the outside, and the setting up of co-educational delinquent centres in which young miscreants of opposite sexes were permitted to cohabit. In 1973, Norway was the first country to make it illegal to strike a child, and in 1981 the Norwegian government was the first to appoint an ombudsman solely responsible for dealing with children's complaints of injustice.

The appointment of ombudsmen—independent investigators of public grievances—is one of the most widely imitated Scandinavian innovations.

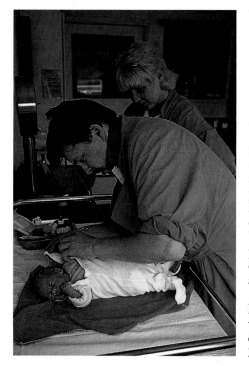

In a hospital in Espoo, a city near Helsinki, a father swaddles his newborn child while his wife looks on. The city's advanced social health facilities enable husbands to attend courses in baby care that prepare them to share the responsibilities of post-natal care.

Since the 1960s, it has given a new word to many languages and provided millions of people with means of appealing against unjust or arbitrary bureaucracy. The position originated in Sweden in 1809, when the duties of the official—properly known as the *justitieombudsman* and commonly called "the JO"—were expressly to see that judges and other public officials acted fairly and impartially. Now the pressure of work is so great that since 1976 it has been split between four officers. In addition, Sweden has four supplementary offices of appeal, covering business and trade, consumer protection, the press and equal opportunities.

The Swedish ombudsmen receive thousands of written submissions a year (a letter need only be addressed "JO Stockholm" to be safely delivered) and every complaint, however trivial, must be investigated. Among the most difficult to assess are the many received from patients in mental hospitals. But even here, the JO may be able to right some injustice. In the 1960s, the then JO, Alfred Bexelius, told an interviewer about a complaint he had received from an alcoholic and wife-beater who had been confined to a mental institution for eight months because the examining doctor considered alcoholism to be a mental disease. A prison sentence for wife-beating would have been shorter. Bexelius commented, "I personally don't like this man, but I will ask the government to compensate him for the extra time he was confined. It's important that society admits a fault."

Scandinavia has also been a world leader in the pursuit of equal rights for women. In 1906, Finland was the second country in the world—after New Zealand—to grant women electoral equality with men. In 1947, Denmark was the first Christian country to allow women to be ordained as priests in its state church, thus setting an example which has been followed by all the Nordic countries with the exception of Finland. Later, Sweden encouraged female employment by offering wage subsidies to companies in which women employees make up 40 per cent or more of the total staff.

Scandinavian women have been conspicuously successful in the political arena. In the mid-1980s, the proportion of women in the various Nordic parliaments was 31 per cent for Finland, 28 per cent for Sweden, 26 per cent for Norway, 24 per cent for Denmark and 15 per cent for Iceland. In 1980, Iceland had the world's first popularly elected woman head of state. The new president, Vigdis Finnbogadottir, had earlier set another major precedent—as one of the first single women in Iceland to win the legal right to adopt a child.

While Scandinavian countries have continually sought new ways to improve the quality of life, they have also been alert to blocking external influences that might conceivably debase existing values. Of all the Nordic states, none has more sternly resisted the encroachments of the outside world than Iceland, a country which has experienced so little immigration that it can be said without much exaggeration that all of its inhabitants are distantly inter-related. Here, tradition dies extremely hard—a fact reflected by the curiously rigid, centuries-old custom of allotting people's names. Icelandic women keep their maiden names after marriage. Children's surnames are composed of the possessive form of the father's Christian name suffixed by *son* ("son") or *dottir* ("daughter") as appropriate. Thus, a husband might be named Njal Sigurdursson, his wife Vigdis Johnsdottir and their children Thor Njalsson and Bryndis Njalsdottir. It is a custom that makes for considerable confusion—if not awkward misunderstandings—when an Icelandic family registers at a hotel abroad. Furthermore, so many names are identical that the Icelandic telephone directory has

5

to include the profession of each subscriber to help identification.

In 1964, the British poet W. H. Auden wrote of Iceland:

Fortunate island
where all men are equal
but not vulgar—not yet.

The comment is still valid today. The spirit of egalitarianism is so genuine that only two people—the president and the island's Lutheran bishop—are addressed by their titles. Iceland remains a nation without a monarchy or an aristocracy of any kind; in essence, a classless society without significant divisions by way of wealth, education or family background. As for vulgarity, it is still resisted by official measures that are designed to safeguard the purity of the ancient Icelandic language and to preserve the highest traditions of Icelandic culture.

For example, the 3,000-strong American NATO base at Keflavik is seen as a threat to Iceland's traditional way of life, and is subject to strict controls. Uniforms are not allowed to be worn off base. An 11.30 p.m. to 6 a.m. curfew is applied to all lower ranks. And the Americans' television station, transmitting 24 hours a day, was converted to cable transmission following Icelandic objections that it was "an unacceptable invasion of national life". By the same token, Icelandic television is restricted to about five hours of transmission a day with Tuesday as a "family day" of complete rest. Until 1984, screens also used to remain blank throughout July, when the majority of people take their summer holiday.

In this way, Icelanders have avoided domination of their leisure hours by television, a medium which, in many countries, seems to have gained the importance of a life-support machine.

They are able to devote more time to creative, cultural and sporting activities. Most especially, they maintain their reputation for being avid readers. "Better shoeless than bookless" goes an old proverb. On a per capita basis, Iceland probably has more bookshops than any other country in the world. Although there are only a quarter of a million inhabitants, some 40 new books are published every month. There are also art galleries, a national theatre and an opera company—all heavily subsidized by the state. And the government further promotes culture by paying salaries to outstanding artists, writers and composers.

Among other Nordic nationals, the Norwegians are perhaps the most protective of their own culture and old values. When the people shocked their government in a 1972 referendum by voting against membership of the EEC, one of the reasons was a vague fear that it might somehow undermine the traditional lifestyle of close-knit agricultural and fishing communities. In the same way, not all Norwegians were overjoyed in the 1970s when the rising price of oil suggested that their country might soon be achieving the highest standard of living in the world. Instead, there were fears that Norway's oil riches would disturb the social framework by inflating the economy, destroying long-established, small-scale industries which would be unable to compete for skilled labour, and debasing the simple, non-materialistic virtues of rural life.

Many Norwegians argued that the new riches from "black gold" should be used to improve the quality of life, to keep unemployment down, and to help Third World countries, rather than to finance flashy development projects

A "FREE CITY" IN THE HEART OF COPENHAGEN

In 1971, when the Danish army moved out of quarters in the Christianshavn district of Copenhagen, their old barracks were gradually occupied by squatters who renamed the area the "Free City of Christiania". In the abandoned military compound they established a largely self-sufficient community with a bohemian lifestyle that attracted craftsmen and artists as well as drifters.

As the fame of Christiania spread, its floating population swelled to about 1,000, including many short-stay foreign visitors. Since 1972, it has gained a degree of official recognition by paying token rent to the Ministry of Defence. But its existence remains highly controversial. Swedish and Norwegian authorities as well as Danes have claimed that Christiania is the major Nordic marketplace for hashish and other drugs, and demands for its closure have frequently been made at Nordic Council meetings.

Residents relax by a half-built mill.

144

An elaborate mural incorporating Buddhist and North American Indian motifs covers a wall in Christiania.

A painted sign indicates the colony entrance.

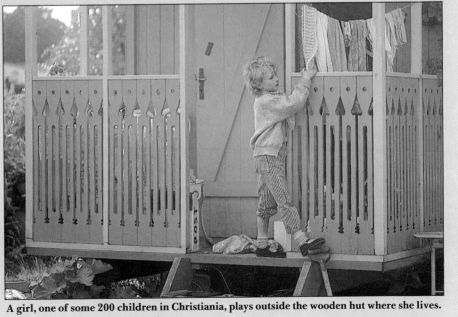

A girl, one of some 200 children in Christiania, plays outside the wooden hut where she lives.

5

and create a wealthy élite. The new-found revenue from oil and natural gas allowed generous government support for any flagging industries and unlimited investment in new ones. As a result, the unemployment rate in Norway in the mid-1980s was among the lowest in Europe, and many of the small, uneconomic communities were saved from extinction by heavy subsidization of local activities.

The other Nordic countries have been less conservative than Norway and Iceland in seeking to preserve traditional ways and values; all, however, have been extremely active in striving to protect their natural environment. Scandinavians have become especially anxious about the development of nuclear power. Only Sweden and Finland have built nuclear reactors, and now Sweden is committed to closing down its plants by the year 2010. This represents a colossal sacrifice on the part of a country which has virtually no coal or oil resources but, ironically, has the largest uranium deposits in Europe. A few years ago, a parliamentary committee estimated that the cost to Sweden of phasing out nuclear power would be in the region of 5 to 10 billion kronur annually for each year the reactors could have been used after the cut-off date.

Opposition to the production of nuclear weapons has been equally strong. The Scandinavians are technically capable of developing these tools of mass destruction, but all five countries have signed and ratified the 1963 Test Ban Treaty and the Non-Proliferation Treaty; the latter was concluded in 1968 by Britain, the Soviet Union and the United States to cut the spread of nuclear weapons. Finland hosted the first East-West Strategic Arms Limitation Talks in 1970 and has championed

a proposal for creating a nuclear-free zone in Scandinavia. Denmark and Norway, though members of NATO, have refused to have nuclear weapons deployed on their soil in peacetime. Sweden, despite the fact that it is extremely defence-conscious (it has one of the most powerful air forces in the world), has formally and unilaterally renounced all nuclear, chemical and biological weapons.

Not content with trying to protect their environment and promote social well-being, the Scandinavians have also consistently concerned themselves with the welfare of the world at large. They have devoted exemplary sums of money to aiding underdeveloped countries, and provided troops for many of the United Nations' peace-keeping operations. Rightly or wrongly, some Nordic countries have spoken out loudly on major world foreign-policy issues.

Sweden's forthright condemnation of the United States' intervention in Vietnam attracted hundreds of American deserters and draft-dodgers to its shores. And Denmark, ever vigilant in the cause of human rights, now operates a rehabilitation and research centre for torture victims which has helped people from as far apart as Argentina and Afghanistan.

Furthermore, no other group of countries has produced so many men of stature to serve as international peacemakers and mediators. One such was the celebrated Norwegian explorer, Fridtjof Nansen, who led his country's delegation to the first assembly of the League of Nations in 1920 and subsequently won worldwide renown as a humanitarian and diplomat. He particularly involved himself in famine relief and the repatriation of prisoners of war, and was responsible for the introduc-

Youngsters practise double-fisted backhands at the Royal Tennis Club in Stockholm. Since Björn Borg's success in the 1970s, Sweden's unrivalled facilities, including 1,400 indoor courts, have made it the strongest tennis nation, per capita, in the world.

tion of the "Nansen Passport", an internationally accepted identity card for displaced and stateless persons.

Among the many Scandinavians who followed Nansen's example was Count Folke Bernadotte, a nephew of King Gustav V of Sweden. As leader of the Swedish Red Cross, he arranged the exchange of many thousands of World War II prisoners; then, in 1948, he was assassinated while attempting, on behalf of the United Nations, to mediate between Jews and Arabs in Palestine. Two of his contemporaries were Norway's Trygve Lie, first Secretary General of the United Nations, and Raoul Wallenberg, the Swedish diplomat who saved the lives of an estimated 100,000 Jews when stationed in Nazi-occupied Budapest, and who disappeared mysteriously following his arrest by Soviet troops in January 1945. Another possibly martyred Swede was Dag Hammarskjöld, also a United Nations Secretary General, who was killed in an air crash in 1961 while on a peace mission to the Congo.

Scandinavians, then, have much to be proud of. In 1965, a newspaper article by Henrik Stangerup, a Danish writer, summarized Nordic progress in glowing terms that reflected the optimism of a great many people at that time:

"We are experiencing today in Scandinavia one of the most important experiments of world history. That may sound pretentious, yet it isn't. Scandinavia of today is the world's avant-garde society. What is taking place among us will happen in other countries tomorrow, as soon as they have reached a comparable level of freedom and welfare. We have an almost unlimited freedom of speech and freedom of the press. We have a standard of living that is the envy of the whole world. We simply have every imaginable opportunity to lead our lives in free development of our human and creative possibilities... If we only know how to use our freedom and to realize it in our lives, our experience... will be of profit to the entire world around us."

Scandinavian self-esteem was then probably at its highest—and justifiably so. The social progress of the Nordic countries had been truly remarkable and was much envied by most foreign observers. But the enthusiasm was already by no means unanimous. From the mid-1950s onwards, in some Western countries, there had been a growing volume of adverse comment on the world's most advanced welfare states.

Such sniping was encouraged in 1959 when U.S. President Dwight Eisenhower publicly referred to an unnamed Scandinavian country that was engaged, he said, in an "experiment in almost complete paternalism", a form of total welfare which, he claimed, had undermined the moral fibre of the whole nation and resulted in large-scale drunkenness and suicide. His speech was bitterly condemned all over Scandinavia; later, on a visit to Sweden, the President, admitting that he had got his facts wrong, publicly apologized. But the charges had taken root, and thereafter sections of the foreign press consistently focused less on Scandinavian enlightenment and more and more on signs of moral decline.

To a degree, the Scandinavians—or more precisely the daringly progressive Swedes and Danes—invited sensational publicity abroad by their far-ranging efforts to free sexuality from the fears and repressions of the past. During the

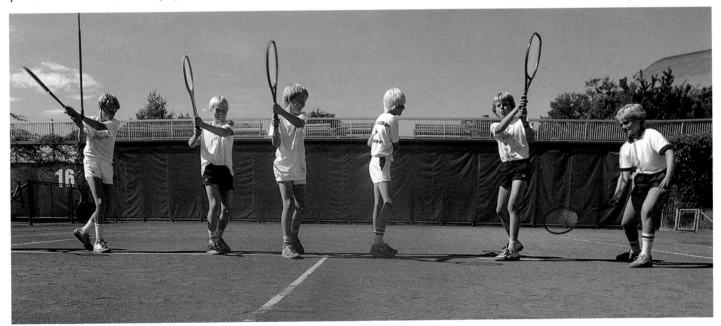

COLLECTIVE LIVING IN A DANISH COMMUNE

In 1978, eighty-five Danes seeking a viable alternative lifestyle pooled their resources to buy a 460-hectare estate at Svanholm, 50 kilometres west of Copenhagen. They dedicated their new community to the principles of collective decision-making, shared responsibility between the sexes and ecological food production. Today, Svanholm has about 100 adult members, plus about 80 children, making it the largest commune in Denmark.

The residents live in small groups of between five and 20 adults in dwellings scattered across the estate. Meals are taken together in the single, large kitchen, and children are cared for in a day nursery while their parents are at work.

Only a third of the adults have jobs outside the commune; the rest work on the estate itself in a wide range of occupations—growing crops, managing the forest and garden, raising farm animals, rabbits and honey bees, producing pinewood furniture from the commune factory and tools from the forge. Mechanically minded residents service the jointly owned cars; others maintain the buildings. Creative skills, too, are utilized and small workshops turn out candles, ceramics and leather goods.

In keeping with the prevailing collectivist philosophy, all income from the sale of produce and services is pooled into one treasury. From this fund, expenses are paid, including mortgage debts, investments, union subscriptions, doctors' bills and small personal allowances for each resident.

In one of the commune's bathrooms, a toothbrush rack bears the names of more than a dozen residents.

In the sewing room, two women patch garments with scrap materials. Residents leave discarded clothes on the shelves for other members to wear or to use for mending.

A woman takes her turn on duty in the cafeteria, which can accommodate about 200 people at one sitting. Hot and cold meals are served every lunchtime and evening.

1960s, when the advent of the contraceptive pill heralded the dawn of a new permissive age, Sweden set the pace by reducing taboos on sex before marriage and making sex education compulsory in schools from the age of 12. More controversially, in 1970, Denmark was the first country to legalize pornography. Sweden soon followed Denmark in abolishing censorship and subsequently tourists flocked to Copenhagen and Stockholm to see live sex shows, porn shops, pseudo-massage parlours, and cinemas and bookshops offering fare unobtainable in other countries.

By the mid-1970s, it was clear that such measures were a mixed blessing. Contrary to expectation, sex crimes increased; prostitution flourished; and the Copenhagen porn trade became a centre for gangsters, pimps, drug-pushers and petty criminals. The result was a moral backlash against the extremes of the permissive age that led to the banning in Denmark and Sweden of live sex shows and child pornography.

Far more ominous for the well-being of society than the excesses of permissiveness, however, were developments following the world oil crisis of 1973. Alone of the Scandinavian nations, Norway was eventually able to benefit, as a producer in the North Sea fields, from the dramatic rise in energy prices that it triggered. Elsewhere, the great Nordic experiment was suddenly subjected to the harsh light of economic duress, and serious weaknesses began to show. Strikes were more frequent; welfare frauds and tax-dodging became commonplace; and the Scandinavians themselves began to question the wisdom of trying to maintain their costly social programmes.

The new concerns manifested themselves in different ways in the different countries. In Denmark, a tax lawyer called Mogens Glistrup unexpectedly became something of a hero. He had defiantly proclaimed on television that he had a personal income of five million kroner (some $700,000) and yet, through a cunning manipulation of the nation's tax laws, he had made no contribution at all to the national revenue. Glistrup won the admiration of hundreds of thousands of Danes who shared his view that enterprise was being stifled by the demands of a voracious welfare state.

Glistrup formed a political party whose main objectives were the reduction of income tax and a massive cutback in welfare expenditure. In 1973, his Progress Party won 28 seats, making it the second largest group in the *Folketing* (parliament). This ground was largely lost by the 1981 elections; by then, the charismatic Glistrup was involved in a complicated law suit that led to his expulsion from parliament and a three-year jail sentence for tax fraud. Nevertheless, his few years of glory were generally regarded as evidence that a large proportion of the Danish people felt that their welfare system had become too expensive and that there was too much bureaucracy and government interference.

Meanwhile, Swedish passions had been stirred by an equally well-publicized case. In January 1976, a rehearsal of Strindberg's *Dance of Death* at Stockholm's Royal Dramatic Theatre ended abruptly when police arrived and ordered its director, the celebrated film-maker Ingmar Bergman, to accompany them immediately to a tax court of inquiry. At the same time, the tax authorities searched Bergman's

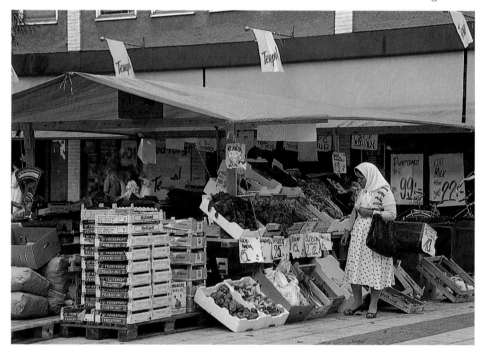

A Turkish woman (*above*) shops at a market stall in the Stockholm suburb of Rinkeby while, nearby, immigrant children (*right*) gather at an outdoor café. One in eight of Sweden's 8.3 million people is either foreign-born or first-generation Swedish.

house and that of his lawyer, and confiscated various documents. The following month, Bergman was officially charged with tax evasion and "careless income tax returns".

The Bergman case became the subject of massive debate in the press, on the radio and on television, especially after an official investigation had cleared Bergman of wrong-doing and led to him receiving a large tax refund from the authorities. Prime Minister Olof Palme telephoned the director personally to express his regrets at the clumsy way the case had been handled. But Bergman was not easily mollified by such apologies. After spending some time in hospital recovering from what he described as "nearly unbearable humiliation", he announced that he was leaving Sweden to work abroad. Before his departure, he savagely attacked

what he called the "ideology of grey compromise" of the Social Democrats, who proclaimed the virtue of costly social reform while ignoring the destructive effects of a bureaucracy spreading "like a fast-growing cancer".

The *cause célèbre* came as a grim reminder of the intrusive powers of Sweden's highly regimented bureaucracy. Income tax inspectors have the power to enter the offices of taxpayers without any warning and can search private homes once they have obtained a court order. They may also obtain details of private accounts from banks. But the controversy surrounding the Bergman case spotlighted an equally significant fact: that the public at large was automatically sympathetic to anyone who was in conflict with the tax authorities. Deep down, many respectable citizens considered that tax evasion was not a

crime but a natural response to unreasonable demands by the state.

Soon after the Bergman trial, the high rate of taxation again came under public attack when Astrid Lindgren, a best-selling author of children's stories, was advised that she must pay the tax board 102 per cent of her 1976 income. This absurd demand was the result of bad mathematics and an anomaly in the way that taxes were charged. The author responded by contributing to the newspaper *Expressen* a charming story about a never-never land where logic could be manipulated to enable people to obtain as many per cents as they wanted.

More sensationally still, in 1983, Ove Rainer, Sweden's Minister of the Judiciary, was accused by a newspaper of paying minuscule taxes on a personal income of more than two million kronur. It emerged that, like thousands of other citizens, he had acted within the law in exploiting a loophole in the tax regulations. In this case, however, Rainer was forced to resign from his government position because morally he had become an embarrassment to the Social Democrats.

By now, to greater or lesser degrees, people in all the five Nordic countries felt heavily burdened by taxation; and throughout Scandinavia the response was a steady growth of the so-called underground or barter economy: a Norwegian accountant gives his services free to a client in exchange for having his cabin cruiser painted. A Finnish builder repairs a lawyer's roof in exchange for free advice. A Swedish doctor gives a motor mechanic a consultation in exchange for having his car serviced. Similarly, in Iceland and Denmark during the early 1980s it was difficult to get private work done

5

without resorting to paying for services in unrecorded cash.

High welfare costs were beginning to weaken the entire Nordic economy. In Sweden, for example, employment was affected as social insurance payments for staff became an intolerable burden for many small businesses. Restaurants, hotels and building firms cut their salaried labour force to an absolute minimum, preferring to sub-contract work where possible. Small shops asked customers whether they wanted a receipt or not; if the answer was no, the shopkeeper could illegally save on purchase-tax payments. Generous sick pay almost equal to normal wages was a disincentive to labour. A study by the Employers' Federation revealed that Sweden's industrial workers had the highest rate of sick leave in the world, and that fully 10 per cent of the work force was continually absent.

Dr. Gunnar Myrdal, 1974 Nobel prize winner in economics, claimed that the tax system was "turning Swedes into a gang of hustlers" and "making nine out of ten Swedes criminals". Quite simply, the idealism and public spiritedness which had built up the Scandinavian welfare society had begun to give way to rampant self-centredness and self-interest.

"The core of the crisis," wrote Bent Rold Andersen, a former Danish Minister of Social Affairs, "is that the ordinary citizen not only openly and without compunction takes part in the underground economy and exploits the system of public services, but also hails others who do, and sees any attempts by the authorities to restrain this tendency as an infringement of his rights."

In 1984, the Swedish novelist Per Olov Enquist summed up his country's dilemma: "In Sweden they dreamt of being able to produce the good human being by legislation; or more precisely, of legislating evil out of existence. It was no bad dream created by wicked people. It developed out of a Christian, a Lutheran, sense of responsibility: *Am I not my brother's keeper?* The problem arose when the sense of responsibility for one's neighbour drove the society to take too much responsibility away from him: he then lacked responsibility, and the society acquired the power."

Enquist might have been describing the experience of Scandinavia as a whole. To varying degrees, all of the Nordic countries had striven by way of legislation to create a more just and humane society. But they never had a sure formula to follow. In drawing up a balance-sheet of their successes and failures, it is important to avoid the temptation of overemphasizing the inevitable mistakes. The Scandinavians are so self-critical and analytical that it is easy for outsiders to catalogue the many shortcomings in their welfare states. The Nordic countries provide an abundance of statistics that chart increase in crime, alcoholism, drug-taking, divorce and suicide. The fact that many other Western countries have experienced far greater increases is not seen by them as a redeeming factor. They set their own high standards of acceptable behaviour and here lies another Nordic paradox: while the Scandinavians have a reputation for being extraordinarily permissive in matters pertaining to sexual liberation, they are, in other ways, unusually restrictive and somewhat puritan.

Alcohol, for example, has long been regarded as the great enemy of the people. Between 1917 and 1955, Swedes could only buy liquor if they had ration books, and these were not granted to married women, citizens under 25 years old or known alcoholics. In the 1920s, Finland introduced total prohibition with disastrous results: as in America, consumption multiplied and illegal production and bootlegging boomed. Now the war on the "evil spirits" is waged by way of extremely high prices and rigid licensing hours in all the Scandinavian countries except Denmark. Drink is distributed through state monopolies and drunken driving is severely punished. Convicted drivers may find themselves serving a term in road-building gangs. In one celebrated case, a Finnish cabinet minister—for the law is the same for all—was sentenced to a period of labour on the site of Helsinki Airport.

Despite the heavy penalties exacted, alcoholism is currently regarded as a greater social problem than ever. Swedes point out that their alcoholic consumption per capita is less than half that of the French, Spanish, Italians or West Germans, but nonetheless the state authorities are deeply concerned. The signs, they say, are that people are starting to drink alcohol at a younger age, and drunken driving still accounts for one third of all traffic accidents. Swedish sociologists have also detected a close link between the rising crime figures and the increase in alcohol and drug consumption.

By their own high standards, the Nordic countries have also fallen short in their bid to achieve true egalitarianism. Many inequalities still exist. For example, free university education is available to all who pass their school-leaving examinations, but support grants are inadequate and therefore the system inevitably favours candidates from wealthier families. Then again, legislation on equal rights for women has failed to eliminate sex discrimination. On average, women in all five countries are paid less than their male counterparts. In Finland, women are technically more advanced than elsewhere, and 40 per cent of the lawyers and 20 per cent of the judges are women. But working class and rural communities are still patriarchal. Few men help with domestic chores. On the other hand, women tend to do more of the heavy industrial jobs such as crane-driving and welding, thus giving force to the old Finnish proverb: "The man steers the boat while the woman rows."

In the mid-1980s, the rate of female employment was among the highest in the Western world. The figures ranged from a high of 47 per cent in Sweden to a low of 40 per cent in Norway, as compared with an average of 30 per cent for other countries. However, the record was not quite as impressive as it appeared since a substantial proportion of employed women were, in fact, working only part-time. Furthermore, many women were handicapped by insufficient child-care facilities.

Perhaps the deepest criticism made of the Nordic-style welfare state is that it encroaches too far on the private life of the citizen. Sweden, in particular, has been charged on this count. Critics point to the police's use of television cameras to scan public places for drunks and drug-traffickers; the existence of highly developed computerized systems that keep a detailed record of every citizen's progress and circumstances, including information about health, education, tax and insurance position, credit worthiness and any motoring offences; and the increasing frequency with which children under the age of 15 who are believed to be

An armed policewoman talks to a colleague while on duty outside the royal palace in Stockholm. All Swedish police—including women officers, who comprise about 10 per cent of the uniformed force—are equipped with .765 calibre Walter revolvers.

5

victims of physical, sexual or psychological abuse are separated from their parents by the state.

In 1983, there was a major public controversy over the number of children—roughly one in a thousand each year—who were being taken into care against their parents' wishes. The authorities called an international press conference in order to answer criticisms, but they only heightened misgivings when they explained that the practice was a result of the increasing psychological pressures on Swedish family life. In the light of the wide and hostile foreign publicity given to this issue, Arne Ruth, editor-in-chief of Sweden's largest daily newspaper, *Dagens Nyheter*, wrote: "Sweden has definitely fallen from grace. If the cliché of political journalism in Western Europe fifteen years ago was of Sweden as the realized utopia of industrial peace and social justice, the stereotype of the Eighties appears to be of Sweden as the home of Big Brother."

This view is blatantly unfair. If Arne Ruth's claim were true, the state would hardly choose to discuss its problems so openly, nor would so many citizens so flagrantly defy certain aspects of the law if they felt there was a "Big Brother". Yet even friends of Scandinavia might agree that there is far too much bureaucracy and state control. As Bent Rold Andersen has asked: "Is it good for human beings to be cosseted, to live in a welfare state, protected not only against external risks, but also against the consequences of their own mistakes, incompetence, or even laziness, and to be deprived of the fruits, not only of luck, but also of their own efforts? No one really knows."

Certainly, the Nordic countries still have many serious socio-economic problems to resolve, and others lie ahead. For example, birth rates in the Nordic countries are among the lowest in the world. Will there be sufficient people of working age to finance the pensions and medical care of the post-war "baby-boom" generation when they reach old age? Will it be possible, in time of rising expectations and expenses, to maintain the present far-ranging social security systems without imposing levels of taxation that discourage enterprise?

Such problems lie in the future. Meanwhile, the Scandinavian social experiment has proved surprisingly resilient in face of rapidly changing economic conditions. Significantly, for all the many criticisms of the Nordic-style welfare state, not even the most vociferous anti-tax groups have ever proposed abandoning the system; and though they may differ in their plans for modifications, all the major political parties are unanimous in their wish to safeguard their version of the existing system. "What really matters," says Bent Rold Andersen, "is whether we have succeeded in abolishing poverty and illiteracy, in reducing tensions between social classes, in promoting social mobility, and in dignifying the common man so that he feels on an equal footing with the rich and the famous."

By those criteria, the Scandinavian experiment must be judged a success—albeit not an unqualified one. After more than half a century, Marquis Childs' concluding judgement of "the middle way" is still as valid as ever: "Whatever the future may bring there will remain the record of a people who cultivated their garden, their rocky, remote, lonely garden with patience, with courage, and with an extraordinary degree of intelligence."

Towering cliffs and glacier-bearing mountains rise above the still waters of the Nordfjord near Loen in western Norway. Such forbidding yet majestic landscapes have remained virtually unchanged since the days of the Vikings a millennium ago.

ACKNOWLEDGEMENTS

The index for this book was prepared by Vicki Robinson. For their help with this volume, the editors also wish to thank the following: Carolyn Alcock, London; Nils-Göran Andersson, Wärtsilä Arctic Design and Marketing; Judy Aspinall, London; Kerstin Asp-Johnsson, Cultural Attaché, Swedish Embassy, London; Brit Bartz-Johannessen, West Norway Tourist Board, Bergen; Ola Hiis Bergh, Bergen Tourist Board, Norway; Kaj Björkman, Stockholm; Martin D. Blake, Press Office, ASEA, Sweden; Mike Brown, London; Walter Collins, Oscar Woollens, London; Danish Embassy, London; Sigvard Estvall, ASEA, Sweden; Annelise Fibaek, Copenhagen; Finnish Embassy, London; Finnish Tourist Board, London; Tryggve Fitje, West Norway Tourist Board, Bergen; Karin Fredgård, Stockholm; Christina Guggenberger, Stockholm Information Service; Eva Gustavsson, Swedish Tourist Board, Stockholm; Liz Hodgson, London; Matti Kohva, Finnfacts, Helsinki; Martin Leighton, Hove, England; Jens and Inger Lindgren, Stockholm; Doris Løkke, Norwegian Tourist Office, Paris; Monika Lubkowska, Jonas Company, London; Ulla Nicolai, Christiania, Copenhagen; Kurt Nielsen, Danish Tourist Board, Copenhagen; Gunnar Nørstad, Press Department, Carlsberg, Copenhagen; Norwegian Embassy, London; Orheim family, Mundal Hotel, Fjaerland, Norway; Captain Jaako Pohjola, Board of Navigation, Helsinki; Paul Reeves, Scott Howard Associates Ltd., London; Karl Skarheim, Norwegian Tourist Board, Oslo; Leif Sundman, Finnfacts, Helsinki; Swedish Embassy, London; Deborah Thompson, London; Ari Valjakka, Personnel and Communications, Wärtsilä, Helsinki; Benny Villumsen, Tulip, Vejle, Denmark.

PICTURE CREDITS

Credits from left to right are separated by semicolons, from top to bottom by dashes.

Cover: Steve Lipson, California. Front endpaper: Map by Roger Stewart, London. Back endpaper: Digitized image by Creative Data, London.

1, 2: © Flag Research Center, Winchester, Massachusetts. **6, 7**: Mick Rock, Walton-on-Thames, England. **8**: Digitized image by Creative Data, London. **8, 9**: David Simson, Bisley, England. **10, 11**: Klaus D. Francke from Bilderberg, Hamburg. **12, 13**: Blaine Harrington, Bethel, Connecticut. **14, 15**: Bernard Gérard, Paris. **15**: Digitized image by Creative Data, London. **16, 17**: Bernard Gérard, Paris. **18**: Bernard Gérard, Paris; Blaine Harrington, Bethel, Connecticut; Bernard Gérard, Paris. **19**: Claude Charlier from Agence A.N.A., Paris; Blaine Harrington, Bethel, Connecticut; Matti Kolho from Värisuomi Oy, Helsinki. **21**: Digitized image by Creative Data, London. **23, 24**: Blaine Harrington, Bethel, Connecticut. **25**: Herbert Fristedt, Sundbyberg, Sweden. **27**: Matti Kolho from Värisuomi Oy, Helsinki; David Simson, Bisley, England. **28**: David Simson, Bisley, England. **29**: Herbert Fristedt, Sundbyberg, Sweden. **30–33**: Blaine Harrington, Bethel, Connecticut. **34**: Brian Seed from Click/Chicago; Blaine Harrington, Bethel, Connecticut – Brian Seed from Click/Chicago. **36, 37**: Bernard Gérard, Paris. **38**: Blaine Harrington, Bethel, Connecticut. **39**: Bernard Gérard, Paris. **40**: Maja Coene from Colorific!, London. **41–44**: Klaus D. Francke from Bilderberg, Hamburg. **45**: Klaus D. Francke from Bilderberg, Hamburg – Brian Seed from Click/Chicago. **46, 47**: Klaus D. Francke from Bilderberg, Hamburg. **48**: Peter Juul from The Daily Telegraph Colour Library, London. **49**: Klaus D. Francke from Bilderberg, Hamburg. **50**: Painting (anonymous) from Krigsskolan-Karlberg, Karlbergs Slott, Stockholm, photograph by Torbjörn Heinlaid. **52**: Silkeborg Museum, Denmark. **53**: Digitized image by Creative Data, London. **54**: © University Museum of National Antiquities, Oslo. **55**: Bernard Gérard, Paris – *Oseberg Wagon* from the University Museum of National Antiquities, Oslo, Norway. **56**: Riksantikvarieämbetet och Statens Historiska Museer, Stockholm. **57**: Courtesy of Kungliga Biblioteket, Stockholm. **58**: The Mansell Collection, London. **59**: Oil on canvas 92 × 47 cm by Willem Boy Grh 467, National Museum, Stockholm. **60**: Blaine Harrington, Bethel, Connecticut; portrait of *King Christian II* by Michael Sittow, Royal Museum of Fine Arts, Copenhagen, photograph by Hans Petersen; *Astronomiae Instauratae mechanica* courtesy of Kungliga Biblioteket, Stockholm. **61**: Drawing of *Karl Johan embracing an old Telemark man* c. 1830 courtesy of Universitetsbiblioteket in Oslo; lobby card for film *Queen Christina*, from the Kobal Collection, London. **63**: Oil on canvas *Oldenburg* courtesy of De Danske Kongers Kronologiske Samling På Rosenborg, København. **64**: Mezzotint (engraving by H. Kingsbury) by permission of the Council of the Linnean Society, London, photograph by Eileen Tweedy from E.T. Archive Ltd., London; hand coloured engraving by permission of the Council of the Linnean Society, London, photograph by Eileen Tweedy, London. **65**: Courtesy of the Kungliga Biblioteket, Stockholm. **67**: Painting by Edvard Petersen courtesy of the Aarhus Kunst Museum, Denmark, photograph by Poul Pedersen, Aarhus. **69**: Courtesy of the Turku Museum of Art, Turku, Finland, photograph by Douglas Sivén, Helsinki. **70**: By kind permission of H.M. King Olav V of Norway. **72**: Pääesikunnan Kuvakeskus (The Finnish Army Archive), Helsinki. **74**: Süddeutscher Verlag, Munich. **75**: Ullstein Bilderdienst, Berlin. **76**: Brian L. Davis, Sanderstead, England. **77**: Ullstein Bilderdienst, Berlin – Wide World Photos Inc., New York. **78–81**: Museet for Danmarks Frihedskamp, København. **82**: Steve Lipson, California. **85**: Gert Wagner from Bildagentur Anne Hamann, Munich. **86–87**: Wilfried Bauer, Hamburg. **88**: Blaine Harrington, Bethel, Connecticut. **91**: Gérald Buthaud from Cosmos, Paris. **92**: Brian Seed from Click/Chicago. **93**: Bernard Gérard, Paris. **94**: Blaine Harrington, Bethel, Connecticut. **95**: David Simson, Bisley, England – Herbert Fristedt, Sundbyberg, Sweden. **97**: Blaine Harrington, Bethel, Connecticut. **98, 99**: Bernard Gérard, Paris. **101**: Matti Kolho from Värisuomi Oy, Helsinki. **102**: Steve Lipson, California. **104**: Herbert Fristedt, Sundbyberg, Sweden. **105–107**: Claes Löfgren, Stockholm. **108**: Herbert Fristedt, Sundbyberg, Sweden. **109**: Claes Löfgren, Stockholm. **111**: Klaus D. Francke from Bilderberg, Hamburg. **112**: Blaine Harrington, Bethel, Connecticut. **115**: Steve Lipson, California. **117**: Brian Seed from Click/Chicago. **119–127**: Blaine Harrington, Bethel, Connecticut. **128, 129**: Photograph by Malcolm Robertson, London. The Aalto-designed furniture (manufactured by Artek Oy AB, Finland) was kindly supplied by the U.K. distributors, The Jonas Company Ltd., 42 Shelton Street, London WC2. **130, 131**: Photograph by Malcolm Robertson, London. Jacobsen and Kjaerholm chairs kindly lent by Fritz Hansen, distributor U.K. Scott Howard Associates Ltd., 32 Broadwick Street, London W1. All other chairs kindly lent by Oscar Woollens Ltd., 421 Finchley Road, London NW3. **133**: Herbert Fristedt, Sundbyberg, Sweden. **134, 135**: Bernard Gérard, Paris. **136–138**: Steve Lipson, California. **139**: Brian Seed from Click/Chicago – Bernard Gérard, Paris. **140–142**: Brian Seed from Click/Chicago. **143–145**: Blaine Harrington, Bethel, Connecticut. **146**: Bernard Gérard, Paris. **147–153**: Blaine Harrington, Bethel, Connecticut. **155**: Dick Rowan, Monterey, California.

BIBLIOGRAPHY

BOOKS

Allen, Hilary, *Norway and Europe in the 1970s.* Universitetsforlaget, Norway, 1979.

Bacon, Walter, *Finland.* Robert Hale and Company, London, 1970.

Baedeker's Scandinavia. The Automobile Association, London, 1982.

Blunt, Wilfred, *The Compleat Naturalist: A Life of Linnaeus.* William Collins, London, 1971.

Bredsdorff, Elias, *Hans Christian Andersen.* Phaidon Press, London, 1975.

Brown, Dale, *The Cooking of Scandinavia.* Time-Life Books, Amsterdam, 1968.

Childs, Marquis, *The Middle Way on Trial.* Yale University Press, New Haven, 1980.

Childs, Marquis, *Sweden, the Middle Way.* Faber and Faber, London, 1936.

Connery, Donald S., *The Scandinavians.* Eyre and Spottiswoode, London, 1966.

Derry, Thomas, *A History of Scandinavia.* George Allen and Unwin, London, 1970.

Elstob, Eric C., *Sweden, a Traveller's History.* Boydell Press, Suffolk, 1979.

Engle, Eloise, and Paananen, Lauri, *The Winter War.* Sidgwick and Jackson, London, 1973.

Estes, Richard J., *The Social Progress of Nations.* Praeger Publishers, New York, 1984.

Fullerton, Brian, and Williams, Alan F., *Scandinavia.* Chatto and Windus, London, 1972.

Graham-Campbell, James, *The Viking World.* Frances Lincoln Publishers, London, 1980.

Graham-Campbell, James, and Kidd, Dafydd, *The Vikings.* British Museum Publications, London, 1980.

Greve, Tim, *Haakon VII of Norway.* C. Hurst and Co., London, 1983.

Handbook of Denmark. Danish Foreign Ministry, Copenhagen, 1974.

Harrison-Church, R.J., ed., *North-Western Europe.* Hulton, Bucks, 1980.

Huntford, Roland, *The New Totalitarians.* Allen Lane, London, 1971.

John, Brian S., *Scandinavia, a New Geography.* Longman Group, London, 1984.

Jones, Mervyn, *The Sami of Lapland.* Minority Rights Group, London, 1982.

Jones, W. Glyn, *Denmark.* Ernest Benn, London, 1970.

Klinge, Matti, *A Brief History of Finland.* Otava Publishing Co., Finland, 1981.

Lauring, Palle, *A History of the Kingdom of Denmark.* Host and Sons Forlag, Copenhagen, 1960.

Lucas, E.L., *Ibsen and Strindberg.* Cassell, London, 1962.

Magnusson, Magnus, *Vikings!* The Bodley Head, London, 1980.

Magnusson, Sigurdur A., *Northern Sphinx: Iceland and the Icelanders from the Settlement to the Present.* C. Hurst and Company, London, 1977.

Maze, Edward, *Creative Sweden.* Gebers Forlag, Stockholm, 1965.

Mead, W.R., *Finland.* Ernest Benn, London, 1968.

Mead, W.R., *An Historical Geography of Scandinavia.* Academic Press, London, 1981.

Mead, W.R., *The Scandinavian Northlands.* Oxford University Press, Oxford, 1974.

Mead, W.R., and Hall, Wendy, *Scandinavia.* Thames and Hudson, London, 1972.

Mead, W.R., and Jaatinen, S.H., *The Åland Islands.* David and Charles, Newton Abbot, 1975.

Mead, W.R., and Smeds, Helmer, *Winter in Finland.* Hugh Evelyn, London, 1967.

Nordic Statistical Secretariat, *Yearbook of Nordic Statistics.* The Nordic Council, Stockholm, 1983.

Popperwell, Ronald G., *Norway.* Ernest Benn, London, 1972.

Richards, J.M., *A Guide to Finnish Architecture.* Hugh Evelyn, London, 1966.

Roberts, Michael, *Gustavus Adolphus and the Rise of Sweden.* The English Universities Press, London, 1973.

Sawyer, Peter H., *Kings and Vikings, Scandinavia and Europe AD 700–1100.* Methuen, London, 1982.

Scherman, Katharine, *Iceland: Daughter of Fire.* Victor Gollancz, London, 1976.

Scobbie, Irene, *Sweden.* Ernest Benn, London, 1972.

Selz, Jean, *Edvard Munch.* Flammarion, Paris, 1974.

Simpson, Colin, *The Viking Circle.* Hodder and Stoughton, London, 1967.

Simpson, Jacqueline, *Everyday Life in the Viking Age.* B.T. Batsford, London, 1967.

Sjøvold, Thorleif, *The Viking Ships in Oslo.* Universitets Oldsaksamling, Oslo, 1979.

Spencer, Arthur, *The Norwegians, How they live and work.* David and Charles, Newton Abbot, 1984.

Thomas, David, *Henrik Ibsen.* The Macmillan Press, London, 1983.

Tietze, Wolf, *Norway.* Kümmerly and Frey, Berne, 1980.

Turner, Barry, and Nordquist, Gunilla, *The Other European Community.* Weidenfeld and Nicolson, London, 1982.

Wadensjö, Gösta, *Meet Sweden.* LiberHermods, Malmö, Sweden, 1979.

Wilson, David, ed., *The Northern World.* Thames and Hudson, London, 1980.

Wuorinen, John H., *A History of Finland.* Columbia University Press, New York, 1965.

PERIODICALS AND PAMPHLETS

"Basic Statistics of Iceland." Ministry for Foreign Affairs, Iceland.

"Factsheet Denmark." Press and Cultural Relations Department of the Ministry of Foreign Affairs, Denmark.

"Fact Sheets on Sweden." The Swedish Institute, Stockholm.

"Finland: A Special Report." *The Times,* 14 November, 1984.

"Finland." *The Guardian,* 6 November, 1984.

"Finland: a reassessment." W.R. Mead, the Geographical Association, 1983.

"Finnish Features." Ministry of Foreign Affairs, Helsinki.

"Nordic Voices." *Daedalus,* the Journal of the American Academy of Arts and Sciences, Spring, 1984.

"The Nordic Enigma." *Daedalus,* the Journal of the American Academy of Arts and Sciences, Winter, 1984.

"Norway Information." The Royal Norwegian Ministry of Foreign Affairs, Norway.

"Norway." *Financial Times* Survey, 18 April, 1984.

Various articles from *Iceland Review, Look at Finland* and *Sweden Now.*

INDEX

Page numbers in italics refer to illustrations or illustrated text.

Colour separations by Scan Studios, Ltd.,
Dublin, Ireland.
Phototypesetting by Tradespools Ltd.,
Somerset, England.
Printed and bound by Artes Gráficas Toledo,
S.A., Spain.
D. L. TO:2015 -1987